RYLAND
PETERS
& SMALL

LONDON NEW YORK

wooden houses

from log cabins to beach houses

JUDITH MILLER

WITH PHOTOGRAPHY BY JAMES MERRELL

First published in the United States in 1999
This revised edition published in 2007
by Ryland Peters & Small, Inc.
519 Broadway
5th Floor
New York, NY 10012
www.rylandpeters.com

10 9 8 7 6 5 4 3 2 1

ISBN-10: 1-84597-347-X
ISBN-13: 978-1-84597-347-6

Catalog-in-Publication Data is available from the
Library Congress on request.

Printed in China

For this edition:

Senior designer Sonya Nathoo
Editor Andrea Bagg
Picture research Emily Westlake
Production Simon Walsh
Publishing director Alison Starling

Text contributors John Wainwright and Lynn Bryan

CONTENTS

FOREWORD

Wood has a quality that can be matched by no other building material, adding an extra dimension to its surroundings and exhibiting a unique combination of color, form, and texture. It offers a compromise between strength and flexibility, and performs well under both compression and tension. As such, it is well suited not only for making up the structural components of a building frame, but also for use in floors, stairs, paneling, windows, doors, and furniture. When natural wood is treated with wax polish, wood stain, or varnish, the beauty of the grain is a thing of wonder. In a room where the walls, floor, door, window frames, chairs, and tables are made of wood, the various subtleties of color, light, and shade create an amazing array of visual effects.

Many aspects of contemporary wooden-house design have been shaped by the dwellings of our ancestors, whose lifestyles and pastimes are revealed by their legacy of craftsmanship. In turn, modern society will also leave traces of the ways in which imaginations have been stretched, with a fusion of Old World traditions and advances in technology, to use wood creatively in the home. This book attempts to place the wooden house into a historical and social context, revealing its various structural skeletons and different styles of interiors through the centuries, tracing the development of wood as an integral design element in international architectural history, and providing inspiration for anyone who appreciates a natural way of life.

Judith Miller

introduction

From the Middle Ages until the Industrial Revolution in the 18th and 19th centuries, most of the population of Europe and Scandinavia was heavily reliant on locally available timber to construct shelter and accommodation. In rural regions with dense forestation, such as large parts of Sweden and Norway, the Swiss and Austrian Alps, and central and eastern Germany, many wooden houses were built with logs, their walls consisting of round or flat-sided logs secured horizontally on top of one another and usually notched together at the corners. Given the extremely cold winters suffered in these areas, one of the main advantages of building in this manner was the insulation provided. However, in urban areas, and in rural regions where the forests were less extensive, log construction was not a viable proposition — transporting the quantity of lumber required was either impossible, too time-consuming, or too expensive.

Consequently, a more economical method of building with wood was devised. The timber-framed houses built in Europe and Scandinavia before the Industrial Revolution incorporated, on average, two-fifths of the wood needed to make a log house of equivalent size. The walls were built from a series of interlocking vertical and horizontal sawn timbers, which were reinforced with diagonal or curved braces and combined with roof trusses, purlins, and rafters to make the building's skeletal framework. Except where windows and doors were inserted, the spaces in the wall frame were filled with non-structural panels of either wattle and daub, or lath, and plaster or occasionally bricks; roofs were of thatch, tiles, or, less often, wooden boards. The majority of early European wood-framed houses, in which the vertical posts and studs, and the horizontal sills and cross-rails were left exposed, were colloquially referred to as half-timbered. However, later, many of these houses were covered with horizontal wooden boards (known as weatherboards, or clapboards) to protect the infill panels from the elements and provide more insulation.

Although many Native Americans had a long tradition of building with wood, a vast repertoire of skills necessary for the construction of log and timber-framed houses crossed the Atlantic with the European

and Scandinavian carpenters who immigrated to the new colonies of North America during the 17th and 18th centuries. Log and timber-framed houses proliferated in North America. Moreover, considerable impetus was given to the construction of weatherboard timber-framed houses in the early 19th century, when a revolutionary method of construction was devised in Chicago. Exploiting the invention of cheap, mass-produced nails, and more uniform lumber from the mechanized sawmills, balloon framing simply involved nailing the horizontal timbers to the vertical studs. As a result, it became easier, quicker, and cheaper to build wooden houses.

In Europe, the Industrial Revolution coincided with the dwindling of timber resources, resulting in brick construction replacing timber framing as the primary method of building residential houses. In most of Scandinavia and many parts of the U.S., where timber remained reasonably plentiful, the construction of balloon-framed and log houses was sustained by the new efficiencies of the lumber industry.

The new technologies of the 19th and 20th centuries resulted in other, supposedly more durable, building materials usurping the preeminence of wood, chief among these being concrete. However, the discovery that concrete can be prone to disintegration and the generally lukewarm appreciation of its visual qualities led to an aversion to concrete-built accommodation during the second half of the 20th century. This has been accompanied by a widespread re-appreciation of the constructional and aesthetic qualities of wood, and of traditional timber-framed and log houses. The result has been a boom in wooden-house construction since the early 1970s, driven by post-Modernist architects and fueled by consumer demand. To contemporary architects, the primary attraction of building with wood lies in the opportunity to explore the versatility of an organic rather than a man-made or synthetic material. To the home owner, the attraction of living in a log or timber-framed house symbolizes a revival and a celebration of a preindustrial, pretechnological age, in which traditional methods and standards of craftsmanship worked in harmony with, rather than exploited and rode roughshod over, Nature.

architectural styles

RIGHT An 18th-century farm moved from the village of Chatel to near Megève, France. The buildings of squared-log construction have been restored by craftsmen using old lumber and traditional techniques.

LEFT A medieval loft in Telemark, constructed of squared pine logs on a stone base before the Black Death of 1350. These lofts were the first two-story buildings on Norwegian farms and roughly 130 have survived, with about 70 in this valley alone.

BELOW RIGHT A restored 18th-century farm from Savoy, France, built in the traditional way with squared, planed logs— a technique that has changed little since the Middle Ages.

The practice of building with logs has survived in forested regions around the world for the past 2,000 years, despite the development of more refined and less expensive wood-building techniques.

log cabins and lodges

Log buildings originated in the extensively forested regions of northern Europe and Scandinavia, and also in Russia, fueled by practical rather than aesthetic considerations. When hunting could no longer support an expanding population, forests were cleared to make way for livestock and arable farming, and the most efficient use for the felled trees was as building material. Before the widespread introduction of mechanized sawmills after the late 18th century, the easiest and quickest way to build was with roughly hewn logs laid horizontally on top of one another, rather than with the planed and jointed wooden frames and planks needed for wood-framed houses.

Log houses were favored in areas of extreme temperatures since heavy log walls produce interiors that are warmer in winter and cooler in summer than wood-framed walls. In these regions, windows in log houses were small and oriented to the warmer south, often with external shutters. The steep pitched roofs had large overhangs to prevent heavy accumulations of snow, and many were insulated with sheets of birch bark covered with split wooden poles or sod. Large stone fireplaces were stoked during the day for cooking and heating, their long flues radiating warmth throughout the night. In summer, shutters and windows were opened.

Softwoods, such as birch, cedar, spruce, and pine, have always been favored over hardwoods for log construction, due to their rapid growth cycle and the fact that they are easy to cut, shape, and stain. Logs can either be stripped of their bark and cambium (the outer layer of sapwood) or left with them intact. Another key element in determining the look of a log house is the profile of the logs making up the walls. The ends of the logs, where they are notched together at the corners of a house, also contribute significantly to its appearance. Two of the most common log-house roofs are "raftered," where the roof is made up of log rafters laid perpendicular to the ridge log (which forms the apex of the roof), and "purlin," where the roof is made up of logs running parallel to the ridge and supported at intervals by vertical posts.

RIGHT AND OPPOSITE,
ABOVE RIGHT Details
showing the construction of
the walls of two log lofts in
Telemark that date from the
medieval period.

LEFT Here, the overhanging
roofs, supported on simple
wood brackets, help to
protect the wooden walls from
rotting. The windows each
have sturdy external wooden
shutters that help to insulate
the interiors against the
severe winter cold.

**OPPOSITE, ABOVE LEFT
AND BELOW** This lodge
nestles at the base of the
Rocky Mountains, near Aspen,
Colorado. It was inspired by
the log cabins in the Great
Camps of the Adirondacks.
The lodge is built on a base
of massive boulders, and the
coped logs have an infill
of polymer chinking.

Although contemporary log houses are often
ground-breaking in design, the influence of traditional
log buildings, such as the basic cabin of the early
American pioneer, cannot be denied. When the settlers
arrived, about 40 percent of the land was forested, and
this, together with the harsh climate, made log
buildings the obvious choice. The first pioneers'
houses were simple huts and cabins, while later
settlers' built more sophisticated hewn-log ranches,
lodges, and barns. For practical reasons, the building
of log houses should have entered a terminal decline
when mechanized sawmills became widespread.
However, log houses enjoyed a revival in the U.S.
at the end of the 19th century, fueled primarily by
romance and aesthetics. The revival began with the
building of the Great Camps in the Adirondack

Mountains in New York state during the late 1880s. Despite the fact that these lodges were expensive playthings of the rich, their significance lay in their affinity with the frontier spirit. The promotion of the log house as a source of moral rectitude and civic pride was further fueled when, during the Great Depression of the 1930s, thousands of out-of-work

ABOVE A farm complex from Rendalen, Norway, which has been relocated to the Glomdalsmuseet in Elverum. The winter farmhouse, which incorporated a belfry, was built c.1730.

ABOVE RIGHT A squared-log house from the market place in Elverum, Norway, built c. 1775 by a German immigrant.

RIGHT Synvisgard Farmhouse was built c. 1668 in Os, Norway, from hand-hewn logs. The interior of the house was decorated in 1744 by a Swedish artist, with paintings depicting historical and rural scenes important to the family.

OPPOSITE A farm-workers' log lodge built near Elverum c.1830.

The widespread appeal of the log house and its romantic associations has ensured the revival and reinterpretation of various methods and styles of log construction.

laborers were recruited to erect a series of traditional log buildings in America's national parks. During the 1960s and 1970s, the log house was discovered by a new generation wishing to drop out of the rat race of modern commercial and industrial life. The appeal spread to the general population, and in the 1980s many specialized companies were established to meet the growing demand for precut log-house kits, most of which were built as vacation homes for middle- and upper-income families. By the 1990s nearly all log houses were being built as primary residences, and thousands of kits are now exported around the world—even to regions with no tradition of log construction.

Quintessentially British, the traditional half-timbered house, made up of an interlocking wooden frame filled in with wattle and daub, can still be found in many villages in northern Europe.

OPPOSITE The Vicarage in Berriew, Wales, is dated 1616, although it has a later brick extension. The gable on the front elevation is picked out in cusped struts creating a quatrefoil pattern.

half-timbered houses

ABOVE Brookgate is one of the oldest manor houses on the Shropshire border between England and Wales. The earliest part was built in 1350 as a single-range (a structure extending in one direction) open to the roof—except for the inclusion of a sleeping loft at one end, now used as a sitting room.

ABOVE RIGHT At Stokesay Castle in Shropshire, a Jacobean gatehouse stands at the entrance to a 13th-century fortified manor house.

In northern Europe two methods of constructing wood-framed buildings were developed: cruck framing and box framing. In both, large wall frames of vertical and horizontal timbers, usually oak, were combined with roof trusses, purlins, and rafters to create the skeleton. This was invariably preassembled off the site, and all the components were numbered before it was dismantled for transportation to the site. Box-framed buildings were made up of a series of square or rectangular timber-framed boxes, known as bays. All but the poorest houses consisted of more than one roofed bay, with long timber purlins joining the roof trusses of each. Crucks were large, slightly curved timbers; they were erected in pairs joined at the top with a collar or tie beam to form an A-shape. Whereas box-framed buildings were divided by the gable panels between each bay, it was possible to incorporate much longer, uninterrupted spaces within a cruck-framed structure. The drawback was that the size of a building was dependent on the wood available, since several trees of roughly equal height and profile were required to build a house of more than one bay. A technique known as aisle framing combined both methods in the

LEFT Berrington Manor near Shrewsbury, England, is an early to mid-15th-century priest's hall house (the right-hand part) that was extended in 1658. The cusped struts are both decorative and structural.

RIGHT Abernodwydd Farm-house, built in Powys, Wales, in 1678, now at Cardiff's Museum of Welsh Life, is typical of the area. Its frame, infilled with wattle and daub, is set on a stone sill to prevent the wood from rotting; its roof is straw with a hazel underthatch.

The look of a half-timbered house could be dramatically altered by the choice of finish for the wooden frame and the infill panels in between.

same building to increase the overall width. On either side of each pair of crucks, additional posts and framing were erected to form new outer walls, creating aisles along both sides of the main building.

The oldest and most widely used infill material was wattle and daub. Oak staves were secured within each section of the framework, and thin branches were woven through the staves and daubed on both sides with a mixture of sand, lime, chopped straw, and dung. It was necessary to apply several layers of limewash, initially and every couple of years, to waterproof the panels and act as a mild fungicide and insecticide.

Although by the early 19th century more durable methods of building with brick, stone, and cement had replaced timber-frame construction in northern Europe, the timeless beauty of the traditional half-timbered house inspired a range of styles. For example, in the U.S., houses of the 1860s and 1870 featured decorative stickwork symbolizing the structural skeleton of the building, while some American Queen Anne houses of 1880-1910 had half-timbered masonry. However, the architectural heritage of the half-timbered house is most evident in the "Tudorbethan" houses of the 1920s and 1930s that dominate the English "garden" suburbs.

LEFT AND RIGHT Burr Tavern is a white-pine clapboard house, built in c. 1835 in East Meredith on the mail route to New York City. Originally coated with white lead paint, its owner, paint specialist Chris Ohrstrom, has repainted it in yellow ocher.

BELOW RIGHT Wooden shingles of the Buttolph Williams House built in Wethersfield, Connecticut, c. 1715 (see p. 31).

The weatherboard, or clapboard, house is intrinsically linked to the New World, with its name conjuring up images of early colonial timber-framed houses sided with cedar boards.

clapboard houses

By the 18th century, timber resources began to diminish in parts of northern Europe, and brick and stone gradually replaced wood as the primary building material. Yet the abundant supply of timber in Scandinavia, North America, Australia, and New Zealand has insured that in many areas timber-frame construction is still favored over building with brick or concrete. The different regional characteristics of vernacular houses can be ascribed to builders responding to the climate of the land. Harsh winters in Scandinavia led to the majority of timber-framed houses being sheathed in horizontal or vertical boards (weatherboarding) to protect the walls from wind, rain, and snow, and provide insulation.

The practice of siding timber-framed houses with wood has its roots in the Norwegian stave churches built during the 12th and 13th centuries. The custom of applying wood siding to the exterior of a timber frame was widely adopted in Scandinavia during the middle of the 17th century when mechanized sawmills, which appeared earlier than in the rest of Europe, began to produce cheaply and easily the uniform timber required for framing and siding. By the early 19th century, ornamental Dragon- or Viking-style architecture, which incorporated horizontal and vertical wood siding, together with a wealth of decorative detail, began to appear in Sweden and subsequently spread to Denmark and Norway.

ABOVE This merchant's house near Bergen, Norway, dates from c. 1690, with an extension built in the 1840s, when weatherboarding was applied. The front of the house, which faces the harbor, was painted white as a sign of status, while the back was coated in much cheaper red paint.

LEFT Militia House in Kent, England, is a wood-framed structure which was weatherboarded in the late 18th century. The dentil cornice is typical of the area.

During the 18th and 19th centuries, many half-timbered houses in Britain and the non-mountainous regions of northern Europe were also weatherboarded—usually horizontally—for ease of maintenance, rather than having their wattle-and-daub infill panels repaired or replaced. However, once bricks became less costly and more widely available as a result of the Industrial Revolution, many half-timbered houses were encased with brick.

European settlers first established roots on the eastern seaboard of North America at the beginning of the 17th century, and they gradually extended their cultures across the continent, introducing their traditional methods of timber-frame construction, which flourished in the densely forested land. All but the grandest Colonial buildings were made of wood. During the Federal era, the 60 or so years that followed the end of the American Colonial period up until the early 1840s, a tremendous number of timber-framed houses were built. The vast majority of the houses erected at this time were well made and sided with overlapping weatherboards, but the method of construction did have drawbacks. The building of a traditional cruck- or box-framed wooden house was a relatively slow process that demanded specialized tools and considerable skill.

ABOVE The Battery, built to billet sailors training on the Kent coast of England, was weatherboarded at the time of construction in 1873.

ABOVE, LEFT A small 19th-century clapboard cottage in Massachusetts.

ABOVE CENTER AND TOP LEFT The Simon Huntington Tavern in Norwich, Connecticut, was built in 1703 and completely renovated in 1768. The structure is oak post and beam with hand-split laths fastened with hand-wrought nails.

OPPOSITE The Isaac Stevens House in Wethersfield, Connecticut, was built in 1788–9 for a prominent leather worker. While the front of the house, which faces the main square, was elaborate to indicate the owner's status, the back (shown here) was much simpler.

BELOW The Buttolph Williams House was built in Wethersfield c. 1715, although it was quite retrospective in style. The house was constructed on stone foundations with oak post-and-beam structural members and wooden shingles.

RIGHT Chase Hill Farm in Rhode Island, is a one-story "Cape Cod" house built in 1792 and restored by Stephen Mack.

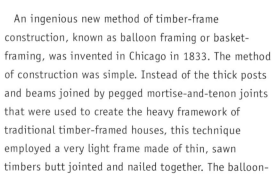

An ingenious new method of timber-frame construction, known as balloon framing or basket-framing, was invented in Chicago in 1833. The method of construction was simple. Instead of the thick posts and beams joined by pegged mortise-and-tenon joints that were used to create the heavy framework of traditional timber-framed houses, this technique employed a very light frame made of thin, sawn timbers butt jointed and nailed together. The balloon-

regional distinctions became less marked, largely due to the fact that most architects copied designs from the same published sources and made use of the same mass-produced building components. Similarities in designs were also fueled by the growth of the prefabricated mail-order house business, and in the 1890s it was not unusual for pre-cut house kits to be transported by rail right across the country.

In many respects the history of clapboard timber-frame construction in the Antipodes is similar to that of the U.S. Settlers brought with them traditional methods of timber-frame construction, and the development of steam-powered sawmills able to

framed house proved to be remarkably durable and made possible the fast-growing, high-standard city and suburban American housing developments of the late 19th and early 20th centuries. Today, approximately three-quarters of the houses built in the U.S. are balloon-framed. Although the initial attraction of this method of building was that it provided relatively inexpensive housing that was quick to assemble, the architectural versatility of balloon-framed houses began to be appreciated and exploited. At least eight architectural styles became prevalent in the U.S. during the second half of the 19th century and up until World War I. Interestingly, however,

THIS PAGE AND OPPOSITE
This lodge-style shingled home overlooking the mountains of the Central Idaho Rockies was designed by Mark Pynn. The home blends forms and materials in a style common to the great lodges of America's national parks, with wood detailing reminiscent of the early 20th-century Arts and Crafts houses of Charles and Henry Greene and Gustav Stickley. The large deep-grooved shingles help to make the substantial mass of the building less apparent.

THIS PAGE In this Brisbane "Queenslander," Australian architect Tony Suttle has exploited all the virtues of the architectural elements traditionally associated with this style of housing. An open deck at the rear and a covered veranda at the front provide plenty of space for the outdoors lifestyle appropriate to the subtropical climate, and the veranda also helps to cool the main body of the house. Additional sub-floor ventilation is provided by the garage and storage space created by raising the accommodation level on stumps that protect the house against flooding.

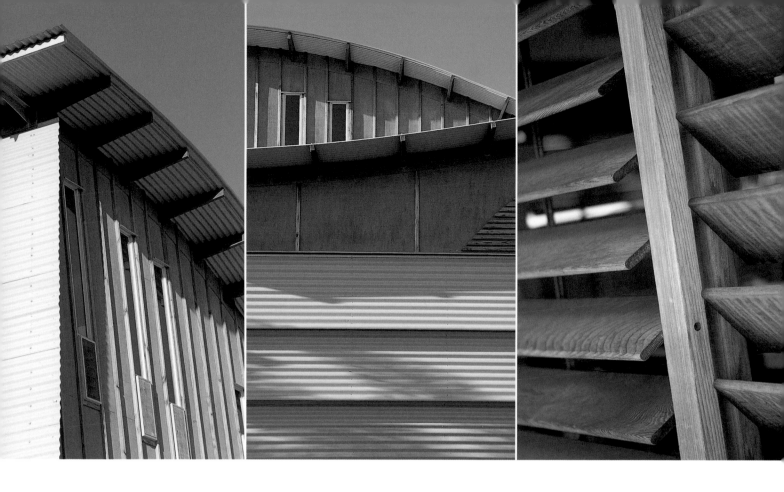

Builders of clapboard houses have not sought to disguise the presence of wood as the primary building material, but instead have emphasized and exploited the structural integrity and decorative versatility of wood.

produce uniform wood made clapboard houses economically viable, particularly when based on balloon-frame construction. In addition, as in the U.S., the development of a reliable railroad network made it possible to transport light prefabricated balloon-framed houses from centers of production on the coast to new settlements inland where skilled carpenters were scarce.

Adaptation to the climate lay at the heart of three important characteristics of Australian timber-frame architecture: the construction of bungalows and the use of verandas and stumps. The single-story bungalow surrounded on all sides by a veranda was ideal for combating the heat and humidity of the tropics, and erecting houses on stumps, or wooden posts, provided protection from termites and seasonal flooding, and also allowed cooling breezes to circulate underneath.

Settlers in New Zealand found a densely forested country, and until about 1890 the majority of timber-framed houses were constructed along traditional lines with mortise-and-tenon joints, rather than nailed butt joints. During the late 19th century, many balloon-framed houses of one-and-a-half storys were built, and in the early 20th century there was a fashion for timber-framed bungalows with verandas, and English-style cottages, some of which had jettied upper floors. Most houses were sided with weatherboards to provide needed protection against the high annual rainfall.

Technological developments in the 20th century have relegated the love affair with the timber house to a small percentage of the population. Yet many forward-thinking modern architects have incorporated wood into innovative designs of breathtaking form.

THIS PAGE The design of Australian architect John Mainwaring's pine-, plywood-, and steel-sided home in Noosaville, on Queensland's Sunshine Coast, is dedicated to sunlight and ventilation. Movable glass walls, sky-lights, a double-height breezeway, louvered windows and doors, and an open-plan layout mean the house breathes and is well lit. The wave-shaped roofs reflect the proximity to a canal and the sea.

living with wood

The humble log cabin, once almost exclusively the territory of alpine farmers, skiing Scandinavians, and colonial pioneers, has an enduring appeal.

log and timber interiors

T he most aesthetically successful houses are those that respond well to the surroundings in which they are built, and log houses, particularly those in forested regions, appear literally to rise out of the land. Of all the vast array of architectural styles of log construction around the world, it is the colder-climate log houses that we most fondly recall, with the romance and nostalgia for a past way of life that they evoke: the alpine chalet or the Scandinavian farmhouse, often thickly coated with snow, the American wilderness cabin high up in the forested mountains or on the open prairie. At the root of the timeless appeal of the log house lies a fundamental truth: spirit of place is everything. With this form of architecture it is easy to create a living environment where there is little change in going from the woods into a traditional log cabin. This harmonious integration of interiors with their exterior surroundings can partly be achieved by the extensive use of glass. French doors and large picture windows

LEFT An 18th-century Savoyard farm that was transported from the Grand-Bornand to Megève, France, and restored by the interior designer Michèle Rédélé. The salon is in the old granary and the loft feel has been retained. The furnishings and small lamps in this living area are by the interior and furniture designer Christian Liaigre, and the theater lantern is from Venice, Italy.

RIGHT The fireplace was originally in another old Savoyard house.

Log houses are a reminder that it is still possible to live closer to nature and to use natural materials.

with panes of glass that reach almost from the floor to the ceiling not only provide extensive views over the surrounding landscape, but also create a greater sense of space and the illusion of an interior that is a part of the forest. It also means that the levels of daylight inside closely mirror those outside.

Important elements in log-built homes are light, space, form, and function, all of which are integral to an architectural style now recognized as Scandinavian. In an historical sense, the style was also well established in northern Europe where there is a great understanding of the relationship between humans and their environment. This is reflected in their interior

design, especially in their sensitive feeling for wood. The basic plan of a log house, whether it is a simple cabin or a larger ranch-style dwelling, features a large, open-plan living room with an open fireplace. Other rooms lead off from this central area: a kitchen, bedrooms, bathrooms, and, in a larger structure, a study or a den. This plan was derived from traditional northern European cabins of hand-sawn logs that were built with a long winter in mind. The main room was the focal point of the house and was large enough to accommodate cooking pots and utensils, beds, chests, and large cupboards, nearly all of which were made of wood. Also essential was a long pine-topped table

ABOVE LEFT The front entrance to this Savoyard farm opens onto the staircase, which leads up to the main living area.

ABOVE RIGHT Many of the log houses built in alpine regions during the 18th and 19th centuries featured a number of external balconies built in at different levels. With balconies that projected some distance out from the sides of the house, carpenters would often key the sides of the handrails into the walls and then brace them inside with tight-fitting blocks of wood.

OPPOSITE The large windows are dressed with heavy jute cutains that hang from steel rings on wrought-iron spikes.

OPPOSITE Les Fermes des Grand Champ in the village of Choseaux, near Megève, are a collection of old Savoyard farms that have been restored by master craftsmen utilizing genuine antique materials from the Maurienne and Tarentaise regions.

LEFT A smoke canopy made from hewn logs hovers above the stone hearth of a sitting room in La Ferme du Chatel.

BELOW La Ferme d'Hauteluce contains many pieces of 18th- and 19th-century pine furniture from the Haute-Savoie.

RIGHT An example of the end of one log wall keyed into the side of another.

Structural elements are in fact a valued part of the visual design.

with wooden chairs or a bench, and a plain, sturdy hutch in which china and glassware were stored. Although practical use, rather than mere decoration, was the reason for an object's existence, everything was crafted with exquisite care.

Color was introduced by means of paint and textiles, and the aesthetic qualities of the walls, roof beams, floorboards, and simple furniture were often enhanced with decorative stenciling, marbling, and folk art. Whether in a log or a half-timbered interior, any scheme to decorate a room begins with the texture and color of the wood on display, and the way in which the walls have been constructed.

In a half-timbered interior, the choice of wallpaper or paint finish for the infill area in between the

The decorative scheme should always complement the wood's natural beauty.

artistic skills during long winter evenings to create warm, colorful, and inviting homes. Decorative folk art was an integral part of Scandinavian heritage.

Despite the advent of modern technology, most of these early style traditions are still practiced, and the original concept remains: practical, simple, well-made furniture highlighted by colorful accessories. The earliest log-cabin dwellers instinctively understood not to compete with the natural qualities of wood, choosing only simple, natural furniture and furnishings, drawing inspiration from their surroundings. Natural yarns were made from flax and colored with dyes extracted from native plants, and then woven into bedspreads, chair and cushion covers, sofa throws, wall hangings, floor rugs, and curtains.

European settlers took their construction skills and decorative traditions to the New World, where they explored ways to exploit the various techniques and effects they had learned in their homelands to create

THIS PAGE AND OPPOSITE In this Elizabethan dining hall, in Brookgate on the border between England and Wales, the cruck construction and other structural timbers are left exposed, and the plaster infill panels are colored with a traditional sienna pigment limewash. The oak refectory table, chairs, and benches date from the 16th century and stand on massive flagstones—the most common entrance-level flooring in houses of this quality. The sitting area is in the original sleeping loft of the single-range building built in 1350.

wooden framework can provide some relief from the dominance of wood. Yet in a traditional log-built structure there really is no escaping the powerful presence of the wood, and of all the forms of domestic architecture, none influences the style of its interior more. Recognizing this, northern Europeans used their

THIS PAGE AND OPPOSITE
A stunning example of folk art (rosemaling) in the guest room of a farmhouse in the Heddal Valley, Telemark, Norway, painted mainly by Olav Hansson in 1782. Hansson was one of the outstanding artists in Telemark and was particularly well known for his religious and secular painting. He was one of the small number of artists who found inspiration in the daily lives and special celebrations of ordinary folk, for example, the figure on the door. Books were also his muse, providing fanciful ideas like the elephant on the ceiling above the box bed. The cupboard was made in 1754 and painted later by an unidentified artist.

extent of the craftsman's artistry: a lamp base made from a twisted branch, smoothed and stained, its gnarled shape displayed to great effect; a sofa frame made of small tree trunks.

As a stage for these decorative elements to be shown off to their best advantage, nothing could be better than a wooden floor. Traditionally wooden floors have had a highly polished finish, but today a pickled effect is often applied for a more natural look. A floor made of stone or quarry tiles, softened with scatter rugs, are good alternatives, as is a natural-fiber carpet in pale brown, stone, or cream.

When a house is on more than one level, the staircase becomes an important architectural feature. A wealth of new technology and materials, which contrast with the wood elsewhere in the room, can be drawn upon to create innovative staircases that curve from one level to the next or appear to be suspended

The natural pigment of paint looks stunning on walls constructed of peeled, round, or flat-sided logs.

homes appropriate to their new environment. Builders experimented with a combination of light and dark wood to great effect, using pale lumber lining to brighten a room, and darker wood for door and window framing to add contrast.

Many early colonial log interiors were decorated with colorful images of mountain flowers and other symbols from a country left behind, but gradually local influences began to be included. In North America, the colorful decorations of the Navajo and other tribes, who drew upon their own rich culture with textiles and furnishings that take their cue from the land, were incorporated. Strong colors, such as red and yellow, blue, cream, and black, representative of the sun, sea, and sky, daylight and nighttime, which dominate the weavings of many Native Amercian tribes, began to appear, together with the signature bold geometric patterns that are ancient tribal emblems. Furniture design also took its cue from whatever objects were discovered outside, reinforcing the link between exterior and interior and illustrating the

THIS PAGE AND OPPOSITE
The interior of this lodge near Aspen, Colorado, shows the influence of the Great Camps of the Adirondacks, especially in the decorative bark, twig, and stickwork on the fireplace. However, it is very much Adirondacks brought to the west. The vast scale of the log structure, with its long vistas and tremendous amount of light, relates more to western-style lodges in Yellowstone National Park, from where many of the logs for the construction were brought as standing-dead timber following a catastrophic fire. The logs were not treated, and even though they have dried out, the heat in the house causes them to settle and crack, sometimes making a sound like thunder.

"Every detail possessed structural significance. Extensions of log ends, coping of intersecting logs and cross bracing of poles became decorative elements." *Andrew Jackson Downing*

in between. Some log houses feature a staircase with gnarled stumps and branches as balusters, logs as newel posts, half-logs for the treads and sawn-off logs as risers. Elaborate newel posts are often created from large logs carved by artisans with patterns inspired by the local environment, depicting birds, flowers, mythical images, or tribal symbols. The fireplace, a focal point in many central living rooms, can either be located in the middle of the room, or on one wall. If set into a log wall, the fireplace can become a decorative feature. A fireplace in the center of a room is usually left open on both sides with a chimney rising to the full height of the ceiling.

Another influential style that developed in log-house interiors and has shaped the design of many contemporary houses is Santa Fe style. When the Spanish invaded Mexico in the 1600s, two very

colourful cultures were combined, resulting in an explosion of decoration. In houses of the wealthy, the flat-plank and log-beam ceilings, built in the traditional Spanish way, were made of the finest-quality lumber. Simple floors, of natural stone or quarry tiles, and stone walls, painted in light tones, provided the ideal neutral background for a vast array of folk art. Santa Fe-style houses traditionally feature ceilings of pine-log rafters, while massive tree trunks support the ceiling and thus become architectural features. The interiors of contemporary Santa Fe-style homes are light and colorful, and filled with a mixture of Spanish and Native American arts and crafts.

One of the most fascinating effects in rooms where wood prevails is the way light plays on the various natural surfaces. Depending on the color of the wood and its finish, light can bring the beauty of the grain to the surface. Contemporary architects and designers working with wood deliberately rely on the almost infinite varieties of natural color, figuring, grain, and texture of the basic building material to create a decorative effect in their interiors. Wax polish or Danish oil, and the patina of age and wood smoke, are the most sympathetic treatments for interior log walls or wooden beams; thick polyurethane varnish should not be used as it prevents the wood from breathing and can give a yellow hue to the finish.

In log-house interiors around the world, it has become usual to line the areas in between the solid structural posts with planks, often painted white, cream, or the traditional Scandinavian blue, creating a wonderful contrast between the smooth wooden lining and the ruggedness of the structural columns.

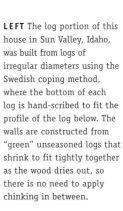

LEFT The log portion of this house in Sun Valley, Idaho, was built from logs of irregular diameters using the Swedish coping method, where the bottom of each log is hand-scribed to fit the profile of the log below. The walls are constructed from "green" unseasoned logs that shrink to fit tightly together as the wood dries out, so there is no need to apply chinking in between.

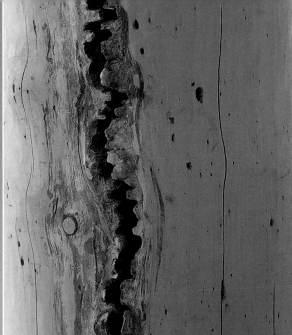

ABOVE RIGHT, TOP AND BOTTOM The vast pine log to the left of the dining area has been struck by a bolt of lightning, creating the vertical split down its length. Character logs such as these are very desirable to architects as they can become a stunning feature, bringing inside a little of the forest's history. The "free-floating" curved staircase contrasts strikingly with the solid log walls.

To create visual diversity, one room may be left with the rounded posts carrying through the rough, rustic look of the exterior, while walls in other rooms, such as the bedroom and bathroom, may be paneled— partially, for decoration, or fully, for greater insulation. Sometimes this decision is influenced by the quality and quantity of lumber available, with poorer quality wood being covered by painted or woodgrained boards. The application of plank paneling enables electrical wiring and heating ducts to be hidden

from view, and also provides relief from the presence of the dominant logs.

Probably the most instantly recognizable log-house interior is that of the traditional American log cabin. From its dusty prairie, hard-working origins, American cowboy style epitomizes the secret fantasy of many red-blooded Americans. Interior designer Thomas Canada Molesworth is credited with creating the style in the 1930s with his remarkable ranch-style Arts and Crafts furniture. He took rural man and elevated the

The large living space incorporates logs, stucco, rock, and glass into an efficient passive solar-heated design that is environmentally and ecologically friendly. There are 6,600 pounds of local granite in the floors; this mountain shale, with 4 inches of concrete below, acts as a heat sink that stores and radiates heat. Throughout the house, walls are either dominated by the irregular but repeating pattern of the warm-colored logs, or combined with plain, white-painted Santa Fe-style adobe portions, which break up the lines of the logs and create a feeling of light and space.

In many respects the ways in which logs are used in Western-style interiors plays a secondary role to the furnishings and decorative details employed.

ruggedness of his lifestyle to decorative heights. Molesworth was master of the burr, described as "an unsightly but benign tumor on a tree." To a skilled and imaginative craftsman, a burr was like a precious jewel that could become the top of a side table or the seat of a stool. The pieces of twig and log furniture designed and made by Molesworth and his team reflected the rustic tradition found across the land.

Molesworth drew inspiration from Native American cultures and used their more recognizable motifs—together with the cactus plant—to good effect alongside familiar cowboy images. Buffalo and steer heads, colorful weavings and rugs, arrowhead curtain rods and pony-skin drapes, wrought-iron chandeliers

and tanned-leather upholstered chairs are the decorative elements at the heart of Western style. Boxes for important documents were covered in leather hide and studded; cotton cowboy scarves were framed and hung as works of art. Lampshades and cushions were also covered in hide, a shining texture to contrast with the roughness of the woven wool blankets used as sofa throws, patterned in typical Prairie style and edged in leather. Cowboy hats, hung on antlers, became design accessories long before the advent of the Marlboro Man and Ralph Lauren. What Molesworth did was prove to many of his peer group that you could embellish the American myth without making it too kitsch—and be successful at it.

THIS PICTURE AND OPPOSITE ABOVE RIGHT
The golden coped logs that make up the bedroom walls provide an ideal neutral back-drop for the minimalist decoration. Their warm tones and texture act as a perfect foil for the floor and the cool white of the bed linen.

LEFT The southwestern feel of this bedroom in a log house in Sun Valley is enhanced by the Native American textiles. The wicker bed and table of silver-birch branches hark back to the Great Camps of the early 20th century.

ABOVE AND TOP The massive chinked pine-log walls lead from the entrance into the open-plan living areas. Pillars of local stone support the maple kitchen surface.

OPPOSITE The entire upstairs area of this lodge in Aspen, Colorado, opens onto the great hall below.

ABOVE LEFT Athelhampton House in Dorset, England, was a high-status home, and the State Bedroom featured a frieze of finely carved oak paneling which was crafted during the Tudor era. The oak tester bed and oak side table date from the time of Charles I, and the bed cover is 18th-century silk.

LEFT The North Chamber of the Silas Deane House in Wethersfield, Connecticut, boasts an excellent example of mid-18th-century paneling.

ABOVE These linenfold panels at Athelhampton House are copies of Tudor originals and date from the mid-19th century.

RIGHT 17th-century oak paneling imported into Athelhampton House from another house. Originally unpainted, the honey-colored oak was painted brown in the 1930s and changed to its present color in 1985.

BELOW RIGHT The colors of the paneling in the Silas Deane House are interpretive rather than analyzed from paint samples. The unusual carved sandstone fireplace was brought upriver from Middletown.

OPPOSITE, ABOVE RIGHT The color of this simple 18th-century paneling in the Simon Huntington Tavern, Norwich, Connecticut, was carefully matched to original paint samples during Stephen Mack's restoration.

Interior walls have always been decorated in some way, and paneling first developed in northern Europe during the 15th century as a means of draft-proofing rooms.

paneling

P aneling came into its own in medieval times when it became widespread in timber-rich areas. It was also common for the framing studs on interior walls to be covered with vertical boards—if oak or fir was used, the wood was normally left in its natural state, whereas a poorer-quality softwood would be painted. In the grander houses of the Tudor and Jacobean eras, the paneling, usually honey-colored or dark-stained oak, would often be applied to the dado or frieze level, or extended to the full height of the wall. Renaissance ideas resulted in an eclectic mix of Classical and Gothic decoration, with motifs such as Doric, Ionic, and Corinthian columns, acanthus leaves, egg-and-dart moldings, and strapwork. Plain panels were often decorated with a carved frieze. With improving carpentry tools and skills, the panels of the Baroque era were larger and featured more expressive and elaborate carvings. A trend for making lesser-quality lumber appear like expensive hardwood developed, and pine or fir panels would be grained to look like oak, while oak might be treated to imitate

walnut. Otherwise, wood was painted one color, marbled, or given a tortoiseshell finish. In the grandest houses, heraldry and Classical architectural themes were often depicted.

Wood paneling remained fashionable as a wall covering until about the mid-18th century, when tapestries, silks, and cotton fabrics, stretched on battens between the dado and the crown molding, became a popular fixture, and the first wallpapers made their impressive debut. After 1760 paneling gradually disappeared from the dado and was replaced

Paneling could be plain and simple, elaborately carved, or made up of intricate patterns of squares, rectangles, and lozenges, with either a flat or fielded (raised) surface.

LEFT Early 18th-century milk-painted paneling in the Simon Huntington Tavern, restored by Stephen Mack.

ABOVE LEFT AND RIGHT 16th-century oak panels adorn the walls of the King's Anteroom in Athelhampton House. The carved stone doorway is also Tudor.

RIGHT A 19th-century fielded-panel (raised-panel) ceiling in an English manor.

by plaster, and it was not until the Victorian period that paneling was revived.

Early settlers in North America made use of many European features, among them wood paneling. Decorative trends from Europe were quickly adopted by colonists emotionally attached to their homeland, but there was a perceptible difference due to the harsher quality of light, and paneling was painted in strong earth tones. Woodgraining and marbling were also used to decorate plain wooden panels. By the Victorian period, wainscoting of oak, mahogany, and native American timbers, particularly maple and cherry, had become fashionable, either waxed or

ABOVE RIGHT (TOP)
19th-century paneling in Athelhampton House, Dorset, England; it is anchored directly onto the early Tudor brick and timber construction.

ABOVE RIGHT In the 18th century, the paneling in the Yorktown Parlour in the Joseph Webb House in Wethersfield would have been painted olive green.

varnished. Olive green, cream, and ivory were fashionable paint colors. In the Art Nouveau period, architects Charles Rennie Mackintosh and Frank Lloyd Wright incorporated vertical paneling in many of their designs, using pine stained almost black. American Beaux-Arts style developed concurrently, and from 1870 to 1920 paneled dados were the height of chic. At this time American colonists adopted Classical and European styles, and drawing rooms, libraries, and dining rooms in the French Classical style featured wooden panels, sometimes with shallow-relief decorative moldings and ornaments in festoon and trophy designs.

Wood is a traditional feature of Scandinavian interiors, but it is the decorative marbled and spattered paint finishes that developed in the 19th century for which Scandinavia is particularly well known.

From the 1920s wooden paneling was seen less on walls across the world. In the 1960s and 1970s architects explored the visual effect of large sheets of plywood. In Britain, tongue-and-groove boards were favored more than plywood, which was seen as the poor man's building material. With the vast array of paint finishes and wallpapers available, wooden paneling is now a rare choice in contemporary homes.

THIS PAGE AND OPPOSITE FAR LEFT When this early Georgian house in Spitalfields, London, England, was first built, the wall paneling would have been painted either a single color, or in lighter and darker shades of one color.

LEFT The Kitchen House, built on an island in a lake in New Hampshire, was inspired by traditional houses on Anguilla in the Caribbean. The high ceilings of these cupcake-shaped houses accentuate the feeling of space, and the skylight situated in the sloping roof increases the amount of natural light that can enter.

RIGHT AND BELOW RIGHT The Bellevue Homestead, Coominya, Australia, is maintained by the National Trust, and is a fine example of an early Australian "Queenslander." The kitchen's simple plank door and the horizontal planks lining the walls retain their original paintwork.

Walking into a room lined with wood is a unique experience because not only is the texture and patina of the timber captivating, the sensual warmth the wood exudes is enveloping.

wood-lined rooms

There is no doubt that an interior paneled with wooden planks has simplicity as the key element. The look and feel of the timber is pervasive, and those who grew up with this natural material cannot live without it somewhere in the house. Regardless of the choice of finish, whether wood is used to line an entire room or simply features in the form of a piece of furniture, its presence dominates an interior and cannot be ignored.

Originally, all cut lumber was allowed to season naturally before it was put to use, so that the raw material revealed its qualities before the carpenter started to work with it. A piece of wood would be selected either for its attractive grain and markings, if it was to be made into a piece of furniture or paneling, or for its thickness and strength, if it was to be used as a framing component or a support beam. Nowadays, lumber is often force-dried in kilns, which can dry the wood too quickly, so when it is used, it absorbs moisture in the

THIS PAGE AND OPPOSITE These simple vertically planked interiors are from the Barfrøstua Farmhouse, built in Rendalen, Norway, in c. 1730 and relocated at the Glomdalsmuseet in Elverum. The addition of plank paneling to insulate the interior of a squared-log construction indicates the affluence of the owner. The furnishings in the farmhouse date from the 18th century.

air, which can cause warping and other structural problems. Lumber that is left to season naturally improves over time, and working with aged wood makes a craftsman's job easier.

When a wooden surface is not concealed beneath a decorative paint finish, with wear and tear its patina becomes smooth to the touch and its homey look is comforting. Unvarnished floorboards polished regularly with beeswax develop a beautiful golden hue; a pine kitchen table treated with a mat varnish maintains its

grain and attractive markings. Yet even plain wood can be painted, either in one neutral shade, or decorated with stenciling or folk art.

All parts of a room—ceiling, walls, and floor—can be paneled with planks, but these can be applied and treated differently according to their location and use to prevent blandness and uniformity within an interior. The planks can be simply butted together, or tongue-and-grooved for a more sophisticated, tight-fitting finish. Ceiling beams can be left untouched, whereas

ABOVE The texture and coloring of natural wood characterize the kitchen in this house in Mount Glorious, Australia. Bark-on trunks support the beams and dominate the room.

ABOVE RIGHT Simple planked walls and doors in the service area of Brookgate, a medieval manor house in Shropshire, England, restored by architect Graham Moss.

a floor or walls of the same wood may be pickled, painted, or sanded, and varnished with a glossy or mat finish. Alternatively, plank panels can be applied sparingly within a room to emphasize or create a design feature, such as an alcove or a shelving unit.

Depending on the choice of finish, wood makes an ideal backdrop for almost any furnishings, from rustic kitchen hutches and elegantly carved antique tables to the most stark, modern stainless-steel cupboards. In most cases, a plank-paneled room creates a less formal

environment than rooms featuring more refined paneled sections, and this informality has a unique charm that is often associated with "country style." The prime source of inspiration for rustic country style is the Great Camps of the Adirondacks. The interior walls of many of these log-built lodges were insulated with beaded or beveled boards that were often laid horizontally so that they resembled hewn logs. The rustic appearance of the cabins was upheld and augmented with decorations, such as thin strips of

OPPOSITE Where fixtures were required for The Battery, a harmonious match between old and "new" was achieved by hunting them down from sources contemporary to the house.

THIS PAGE When artist Marilyn Phipps bought The Battery, on England's Kent coast, she was intent on a renovation that would create a relaxing, spacious environment for herself and fellow artists, while at the same time preserving the original character of a building built by the navy at the end of the 19th century for billeting sailors. Although some of the walls were moved to create additional and larger spaces, the plank paneling was retained and, in most rooms, repainted in the original pale "seaside" blue.

birch bark between the ceiling rafters. "Country style" is also characterized by furniture and accessories of natural, simple textiles and materials that very often draw on a long tradition of arts and crafts. The "country" influence stems from our early ancestors' desire to make their basic homes attractive and comfortable, while fashioning all the furniture, tools, and household objects that they required from a raw material that was easy to work with and readily available in most parts of the world.

The earliest houses were just one large room where a family ate, slept, and entertained around a central hearth. Ceilings were high to let the smoke drift upward, so when the wall fireplace replaced the central hearth, there was room for another floor to be built above the entrance level. Wooden planks were

LEFT The elegant dining room in this house built overlooking a fjord outside Bergen, Norway, is in the oldest part of the building, which dates from the late 17th century. The horizontally applied chamfered planks are an important clue to this date, and the color is original and typical for this area and period.

RIGHT The dining room (see opposite) leads into a later part of the house added in the early years of the 19th century. The locally made clock is painted to imitate mahogany, and the glass painting on the far wall is dated 1841.

As well as for its aesthetic qualities, wooden planking was widely used to panel interior walls for the insulation it provided against the cold.

PREVIOUS PAGE This tiny one-room lodge in New York state was inspired architecturally by a hunting lodge in New Hampshire. The room feels large due mainly to the vast roof construction. The floor area of the lodge is about 30 feet square, and 10 feet of that is porch. The rough pine floor planks vary from 12 to 26 inches in width. Ample storage space is provided by the simple hollow wooden bench seating running around the walls. The rustic staircase with balusters of whittled cedar branches, collected by the Shope family from nearby, leads up to the communal sleeping balcony.

the obvious construction material for these upper-story floors. Before the Industrial Revolution, all wooden planks were sawn by hand and were therefore not of a standard size. Many early houses feature superb floorboards, which vary in width and often slope off to one side of the room. The appeal of these planks is due partly to their irregularity and also to their attractive surfaces, worn smooth and buffed to a sheen by generations of families. Without these floors, much of the charm of many delightful houses would be lost.

In many parts of northern Europe and Scandinavia, where weatherboarding was traditionally applied to the exteriors of timber-framed houses to protect them from the harsh climate, wooden planks were also widely used as a lining for interior walls to provide additional insulation. In addition to being an economical choice, breathable wood also provided a natural means of controlling the flow of air in and out of the house. Everything in the home came from the land and, evidently, wood was not only an obvious and practical choice for house construction, it was also the

A combination of wooden floorboards and plank-paneled interior walls creates an informal "country style" home.

most appropriate material for making furniture that was in keeping with the style of a wood-dominated interior. Not surprisingly, many aspects of Scandinavian and European building and interior design are apparent in the New World houses of North America and the Antipodes. Reflecting the style of their homeland, colonial kitchens of the late 18th century were comfortable rooms that were alive with strong, earthy colors, often provided by painted floorcloths or woven flax rugs.

More Scandinavians colonized America than Australia and New Zealand, and the interiors have different characteristics as a result. Coming from a part of the world with many hours of darkness, the extensive use of bright colors, stenciling, and folk art had become major aspects of Scandinavia's decorative heritage. Consequently, wall and floor treatments were more colorful in America than in the Antipodes, and furniture was more highly decorated. Another reason for the differences in

OPPOSITE The wall of the upstairs hall was the original outer wall of this house built near Bergen in c. 1690.

LEFT The chamfered planks in this 17th-century sitting room are an indication of status and that the house probably belonged to a wealthy merchant.

ABOVE The original color of the kitchen walls was probably a darker gray than the floor, but the bright blue is also a traditional color. The slightly beaded planks show this part of the house to be late 19th century.

TOP The plain planked wall indicates that this sleeping area for guests is in a part of the house added in the early 19th century.

Despite the range of new materials available, wood remains the most versatile.

THIS PAGE The plank paneling in this 1850s house in Rossum, Holland, was introduced by the owner and designer, Ischa van Delft. The decoration of the house is influenced by a mixture of stylistic elements, which complement each other to create a unified interior. Originally a cafe with papered walls, the room has been transformed by the elegant plank cladding, which is painted in a two-tone finish, and it now evokes an 18th-century town house.

decorating style was the fact that European interior fashions reached the Americas long before New Zealand and Australia. In addition, the shorter and less hazardous journey across the Atlantic meant that many families had been able to take their precious works of art, small pieces of furniture, china, and glassware with them, and these initially provided inspiration for most newly crafted items. However, the general style of interiors was less elaborate than in Europe. Through necessity, all objects in the home were utilitarian. Yet an ingrained respect for craftsmanship and an appreciation of first-class materials had been transported from the homeland, and these standards were applied to each new project undertaken. In keeping with the traditions of their homeland, mantelpieces, staircases, and balustrades, and any of the other decorative components that required fine work, were made with careful thought.

Whether in Europe, Scandinavia, or the New World, despite the "country" influence and the prevalence of

LEFT AND BOTTOM
The tripartite division of
the walls extends to a small
sitting room in the Bellevue
Homestead (bottom), but
here the paneling is painted
to highlight the divisions.
The horizontal tongue-and-
groove planking (left) is in a
covered walkway linking two
sections of the house.

BELOW The hardwood
plank paneling on the
dining-room walls of the
Bellevue Homestead shows
the tripartite division of
frieze, field, and dado that
was fashionable in the
public rooms of more affluent
households during the early
1870s, and remained in vogue
well into the 20th century.

Wood painted white can creature a versatile backdrop into which can be introduced vibrant splashes of color by means of fresh flowers and plants.

often quite basic hand-crafted furniture, many plank-lined interiors have a style that can only be described as sophisticated. Vertical tongue-and-groove plank paneling was often an elegant wall covering for stylish townhouses. In American Colonial interiors this elegance was reflected in a love affair with the Georgian, or Neoclassical, influence, which was at its height in the 1790s. Houses were more spacious, with lofty ceilings and large windows, which often extended down to the floor in the French style. Many original pieces of furniture had been brought across the Atlantic by wealthier families, and carpenters found

their skills greatly appreciated in the New World. They became adept at creating replicas of Europe's finest furniture, many of which have become treasured antiques in their own right.

Creating a welcoming home in the sometimes harsh conditions of the colonies was truly a labor of love. Many settlers had an honest belief that plain, simple things were better than anything flashy or complicated in form. Shelter had to be built quickly from whatever materials were available, so the main elements to be taken into account were function and strength. Shelving units were simply painted planks

ABOVE LEFT AND RIGHT The vertically plank-paneled walls and ceiling in this renovated and extended Brisbane "Queenslander" have been painted satin-gloss white.

OPPOSITE AND OVERLEAF The walls of interior and furniture designer Christian Liaigre's 1830s house near La Rochelle, France, were re-paneled and painted—a common practice on the island as a precaution against damp. The salon has a monastic feel, and the furniture, designed by him for the house, is Asiatic in inspiration. The fire surround has a distinctly Classical look with a hint of the exotic provided by the coral.

resting on supports that were nailed onto the wall; early food storage cabinets were made from packing-case material.

The similarities between colonial houses built in America and the Antipodes during the same period are fascinating. Many of these common features of building and design are due to the shared origins of the immigrants who transferred the traditions of their homeland to their new settlements overseas. In many cases, these influences were modified according to the climate and topography of the new environment. One shared characteristic was the appreciation of space, and this was reflected in the light, airy, and uncluttered rooms that are the hallmark of houses in the New World. Although different woods were often employed—jarrah in Australia, Kauri in New Zealand, and cedar in America, with pine used in all areas—the basic house structure was similar. The American porch was echoed in the Antipodean veranda, both of which were designed to provide shade from the blistering sun; wooden louvered shutters were another common feature in the hot regions of both continents; and in colder areas, thick, solid wood shutters built as part of the window frame became prevalent. Across the world, the colonists' movement toward the paring down and simplifying of decoration became firmly entrenched.

OPPOSITE, CLOCKWISE FROM TOP RIGHT A simple planked interior painted in cool whites and creams provides a blank canvas for a colorful collection of artefacts and textiles. This house on Long Island, New York, displays hats from Bolivia, an antique Dutch waistcoat, bags from Morocco, and flour-sack drawings from Santa Fe, and modern Donghia chairs and a table. A light, restrained interior was also created in an island house in New Hampshire.

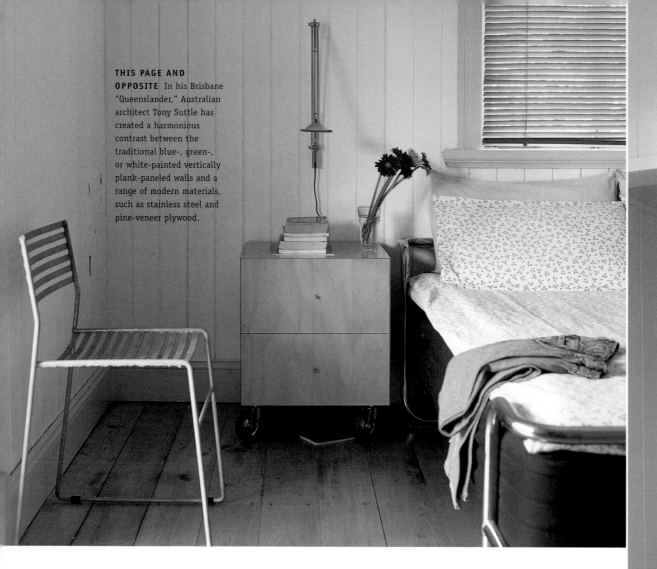

THIS PAGE AND OPPOSITE In his Brisbane "Queenslander," Australian architect Tony Suttle has created a harmonious contrast between the traditional blue-, green-, or white-painted vertically plank-paneled walls and a range of modern materials, such as stainless steel and pine-veneer plywood.

A natural progression was the development in North America of one of the most influential design movements—Shaker style. Established by the sect founded in 1747 as an offshoot of the Quakers, the Shaker influence is largely responsible for the simple, minimalist style of many contemporary interiors. A series of Shaker communities spread from New York as far west as Ohio, and from their ideals came a wish to create a uniformity of style in all the settlements. The final design of most Shaker goods was reached between 1820 and 1850, and everything thereafter was crafted to the same specifications. Everything they made and used was of the highest quality, and Shaker interiors were light and simple. Perfectly proportioned furniture, with simple, uncluttered lines, was designed with its function in mind and an abiding appreciation of the character of the wood chosen.

BELOW AND OPPOSITE
Architect Olivier Vidal transformed this minute pied-à-terre (10 x 26 feet) in the Palais Royal in Paris, France. The walls and surfaces are covered in okoum plywood, sanded and polished to give a hint of sandalwood. The wall panels, reminiscent of the work of Charles Rennie Mackintosh, open to reveal closets, cupboards, shelf units, and a bathroom. The desk turns into a spare bed, creating the feel of a ship's cabin. The only partition is obliquely angled with the desk/spare bed on one side and the main sleeping area behind.

FAR LEFT, BELOW LEFT AND OPPOSITE The walls and ceilings of this family retreat near Sydney, Australia, are made of plywood sheeting (set within steel portal frames). These wooden surfaces, together with the steeply pitched roof, create a sense of living in an Alpine ski lodge.

ABOVE LEFT AND BELOW The guest pavilion that "hangs off the edge" of the house, incorporates two bedrooms and a bathroom, and is reached by a covered walkway. It offers panoramic views of the countryside below and gives the occupants the sense of "sailing in space."

Strong color was a feature of the interiors, with walls and furniture often painted in shades of red, blue, green, and yellow. Windows were usually left bare, and polished wooden floors were often covered with handmade rag or hooked rugs colored with natural dyes. It is hard to identify precisely what followers of modern country style find so attractive about Shaker designs, but it is probably the absence of all the clutter and fussiness associated with Victorian English country style. The movement's influence is evident in the plain, uncluttered rooms of many contemporary country-style houses, which feature furniture with simple lines, pure cotton bedspreads, and natural baskets, often used as containers for magazines.

Modern architects working in Australia and New Zealand are masters of the wood-lined room as a result of a long tradition of working with wood, from which they have learned techniques and drawn inspiration. When the first of many groups of British settlers arrived in New Zealand in 1840, many brought prefabricated houses with them, and others were ordered from Australia. By 1860, the small wooden house was established as New Zealand's vernacular dwelling, providing the basic design from which other architectural styles began to develop.

In modern Antipodean houses, architects and designers have revolutionized the style of wood-lined interiors, often by employing standard plank paneling in combination with a wide range of versatile synthetics and metals, and exploiting new technology to allow the incorporation of vast spans of glass. Many traditional features are still adhered to, but the difference is the improved techniques with which paneling is applied and the choice of stains and paints available to use as finishes. Areas of wooden surfaces are painted white and off-white, pickled or left

In adapting and recreating original elements, the interpretation of modern architects encourages a new way of looking at interior design.

natural, creating solid wall areas to balance the wide open expanses of glass that let in vast amounts of natural light. In keeping with a modern, minimalist approach, plain wooden walls create a neutral backdrop for all styles of furnishings.

The way of life in the "young" countries is less formal than in Europe, and the modern wooden interiors of the Antipodes and the U.S. reflect this attitude. Living rooms are large and open to the world through large floor-to-ceiling glass windows or sliding doors that often lead onto a wooden veranda. Inspired by Shaker

THIS PAGE AND OPPOSITE The main dining and living areas of this stunning house in Auckland, New Zealand, is divided by groups of furniture rather than partitioned off by walls. One of the fundamental design statements is the use of glass for the walls and part of the ceiling, which provides extensive views over the ever-changing landscape surrounding the house.

style, possessions are often hung on hooks or pegs on the backs of doors and on the walls. Furniture is also less formal: chairs are light and portable, and large, comfortable sofas are swamped with cushions and upholstered in natural hard-wearing fabrics. Where the windows are not covered by billowing fabric, plantation shutters keep out the night and the occasional storm. It appears as though a full circle has been turned: despite its European origins, the style of New World interiors is now a key influence in the design of modern wood-lined rooms around the world.

interior details

FAR RIGHT The ceiling of this large 18th-century barn, redesigned and restored by Stephen Mack, is made up of 200-year-old oak roof boards, sawn on a water-powered mill, and hewn oak rafters.

RIGHT Large de-barked log purlins support hand-hewn rafters and butt-jointed roof boards in this restored 18th-century Savoyard log farmhouse in Megève.

BELOW This double-floored attic in the Joseph Webb House in Wethersfield, Connecticut, was the sleeping area for the household slaves. The hand-hewn purlins, rafters, and planks are part of a double-pitched gambrel roof.

The structural frame of the roof formed the earliest ceilings, and today's architects are once again exploring its visual possibilities.

ceilings

Before the 17th century, the structural frame of the roof served as the ceiling in most one-story wooden houses. In cruck-framed buildings it consisted of pairs of crucks, and trusses and purlins; in box-framed structures it comprised beams, trusses, purlins, and rafters. In two-story houses, ground-floor ceilings were the beams and joists that supported the floor above, with the undersides of the floorboards exposed. By mid-17th century, exposed wooden ceilings had begun to be superseded in urban houses by suspended plaster ceilings, and during the 19th and 20th centuries, suspended plaster and then drywall became the most common forms of ceiling, with more ornate 19th-

century examples embellished with rich polychrome colors and gilding. However, wooden-board and exposed-timber ceilings did remain fashionable in many styles of housing. During the 20th and 21st centuries, notable exceptions to the drywall ceiling include tongue-and-groove boards (mostly varnished or painted pine) that have been installed in numerous styles of houses, particularly in kitchens and bathrooms. But the most significant development over the last 35 years is the revival of pitched roofs (often abandoned in favor of flat roofs during the Modernist era). This has allowed contemporary architects of log, wood-framed, and even stone and brick-built houses to explore again the visual dynamics of exposed skeletal roof structures.

ABOVE Pairs of jointed crucks and hewn-log purlins support the roof of 17th-century Kennixton Farmhouse, built in West Glamorgan, Wales. The thatched wheat-straw roof is laid over a woven straw mat.

ABOVE LEFT Built in Dyfed, Wales, between 1760 and 1780, Nant Wallter Cottage has a thatched straw roof laid over a wattle hazel base. The roof is supported by log purlins and two pairs of jointed crucks.

OPPOSITE AND BELOW
In this lodge-style home in Sun Valley, Idaho, architect Mark Pynn has developed a unique wooden roof system with a gridded "structural lattice" ceiling, made of double and fake purlins. This served as the basis for the Craftsman-style detailing which is found throughout the house. The Mission-style geometrically shaped light fixtures are characteristic of the Arts and Crafts movement.

BELOW LEFT In the guest bedroom, wooden pegs cover the steel strengtheners in the constructional wooden frame.

LEFT In his 1830s house near La Rochelle, France, designer Christian Liaigre combines his love of bleached, light-colored oak floorboards, and white-painted plank paneling and simple beamed ceilings with the contrasting textures of oily hardwoods.

Once the upper-story wood floor made its debut, there was no doubt that it would become a stylish feature of any house.

Wooden boards are the most basic type of flooring, but their natural beauty can be exploited to complement many design schemes.

floors

There is nothing quite like the effect of a highly polished wooden floor to enhance the decorative scheme of a room. Depending on the lumber used and the choice of treatment, wooden floors provide the ideal backdrop for many styles of interiors, and complement antique and contemporary furniture alike. The color and beauty of the grain cannot be denied, especially if the planks are merely coated with oils for protection; too much shine is counterproductive and it is wise to remember this when choosing a finish. When early lofty houses were divided into more than one story by the insertion of a ceiling, the wooden floor came into its own. Early floorboards were hand-sawn and, intriguingly, were not fixed to the structural fame, making them a portable feature. From the 17th century machine-cut planks

THIS PAGE Stained and waxed butt-jointed wooden floorboards in a parlor in Stephen Mack's 18th-century, one-story "Cape Cod" house, Chase Hill Farm in Rhode Island.

OPPOSITE Stained
and varnished wooden
floorboards contrast with
the white-painted tongue-
and-groove wall paneling in
this 1920s house, creating
a light, airy interior.

LEFT AND RIGHT The
floorboards throughout this
1980s house on Long Island,
New York, are butt jointed and
made of locally grown pine.

BELOW Bright-yellow painted
floorboards in the bathroom
of a modern extension to an
early 19th-century home.

Easy to clean and maintain, wooden floorboards have an enduring appeal.

became available. Many different woods are used for
flooring, including elm, oak, pine, teak, maple, and,
in the Antipodes, native hardwoods such as kauri and
rimu. Boards may be plain or tongue-and-groove, and
can also be laid as parquet in various patterns, ranging
from herringbone to complicated geometric designs.
Many woods need only to be waxed or oiled and
polished; lighter woods such as pine may be stained,
sometimes a very dark tone. Floorboards may be left
uncovered, creating a stunning backdrop for furniture
and soft furnishings, or serve as a background for
patterned, colorful carpets and rugs. Wooden floors
have an enduring appeal and have remained the
preferred choice of many people, despite the increased
availability of alternative flooring materials.

stairs

Underpinning the functionality of a house, stairs have traditionally also made significant contributions to their style and decoration.

ABOVE Whittled cedar branches serve as the balustrade and small skip-peeled cedar logs are used for the handrails in this Adirondacks-style staircase in a one-room Stick-style cabin in New York state.

RIGHT ABOVE AND BELOW The treads of this staircase in a house in Aspen, Colorado, are made from peeled logs, cut from standing-dead 400-year-old larches killed by beetles or fire during the 1930s.

OPPOSITE The splendid staircase in this house near Biarritz, France, dates from c. 1770. It is sawn and carved to a flatter, rustic version of a more refined, rounded Louis XIII pattern.

The simple ladder naturally evolved into a straight flight of stairs, often fitted into a narrow space and partitioned off. Dog-leg staircases, consisting of two flights at right angles with a half-landing, were also common as they took up a small amount of room. Grand Tudor and Jacobean houses had lavishly decorated staircases, and newel posts even in average houses were turned and carved. A spiral staircase with a large square central newel post of brick or stone was the ultimate in chic, but by mid-16th century it had evolved into the framed newel stair—a wood-framed tower surrounded by a brick or stone stairwell.

Elizabethan balusters (banisters) were turned to look like columns, or waisted; carved and pierced flat balusters were typical of the Jacobean era. Most staircases were "closed string," in which the treads and risers are covered at the side by a sloping member which supports the balustrade, creating a straight rather than a stepped profile. Baroque staircases were massive and usually of oak; the finest featured balustrades of continuous pierced panels depicting strapwork (decoration formed by interlaced strips) or acanthus scrollwork, sometimes with carved figures. Turned waisted balusters were common until about 1650, when the vase shape was favored, and after 1660 twisted banisters were popular.

Georgian houses often had a main staircase and backstairs for servants; apart from the polished handrail, the wood was given a flat-color or woodgrain finish. By the early 19th century most staircases were "open string," with tapering balusters set into the exposed treads; handrails were flatter and ended in a smooth circle on the newel post. In Regency and Victorian England handrails, were often mahogany, and fancy turned balusters and newel posts were mass-

Stairs—from banister-less, open-string internal staircases to simple, bare wooden stairs—can enhance appreciation of the spatial qualities of a house.

ABOVE The stairs in the early 19th-century Burr Tavern, in East Meredith, New York, were originally painted chrome green, but were subsequently stripped. The current owner has repainted them yellow ocher, olive green, and vermilion.

ABOVE RIGHT A boxed, open-string, dog-leg staircase at Stephen Mack's home, Chase Hill Farm, built in the late 18th century in Rhode Island. The risers, understairs door, and tongue-and-groove planking are painted Colonial red.

RIGHT This unusual banister-less staircase was designed by the architect Olivier Vidal.

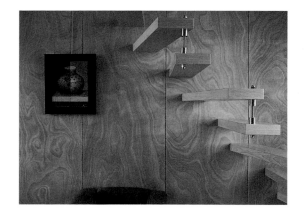

produced. The 1930s saw cantilevered staircases following the line of curved walls, yet it was not until the 1950s that architects fully appreciated how staircases could open up living areas and enhance appreciation of the particular spatial qualities of a house. However, the most significant development in the Post-Modern era has been the resurgence in popularity of bare wooden stairs: displaying the natural beauty of wood, they are also easy to maintain and in-keeping with a prevailing design philosophy that advocates simple, clean lines.

ABOVE LEFT AND RIGHT
A double-dog-leg open-string staircase in the Silas Deane House, built in 1766 in Wethersfield. The highly polished mahogany balustrade, which was produced locally in Wethersfield, has a repeated pattern of two different styles of turning—a fairly common feature of later Colonial design.

FAR LEFT The stairwell in an 1830s house near La Rochelle, France, retains its original paintwork, but has lost its simple balustrade.

LEFT A plain quarter-turn staircase in the c. 1715 Buttolph Williams House, in Wethersfield, Connecticut.

LEFT (BELOW) A narrow stair hall, featuring maple treads and risers and a maple handrail, in a modern house designed by architect Mark Pynn and built into the side of the mountain in Sun Valley, Idaho.

THIS PAGE The 17th-century paneled walls and doors in the dining room of the English manor, Athelhampton House, are made of oak and were painted in 1985.

An external door provides a focal point from which to design the architectural style of a facade and, equally, the design of internal doors influences the proportions of the rooms.

doors

ABOVE (TOP RIGHT) A sturdy, double-boarded (or cross-boarded) unpainted pine door, in Stephen Mack's restored late 18th-century Chase Hill Farm in Rhode Island.

ABOVE Large half-glazed doors divide the entrance lobby from a sitting room in Christian Liaigre's house near La Rochelle, France.

The earliest and most basic doors were made up of vertical or horizontal planks, butt jointed and nailed together. In many wooden houses this simple style has been retained, and often it is only the decorative addition that has changed with the fashions of each passing century. Another early type of door construction consisted of horizontal battens applied to the inside face, known as a cross-battened door, or by a second set of planks laid at right angles to the first—a double-boarded or cross-boarded door. Later, paneled doors, consisting of a wooden framework with an infill of wooden panels, became common and are still popular. There can be anywhere from two to six or more panels, and panels may be flat or raised (fielded). Linenfold paneling consists of wood carved in such a way as to imitate folded fabric and has been periodically fashionable from the mid-16th century. Types of lumber used for

ABOVE LEFT AND RIGHT
These are fielded-panel doors in Stephen Mack's home, Chase Hill Farm. In urban areas, the six- rather than the four-panel door became increasingly common in Georgian houses during the course of the 18th century. The degree of relief on the panels also changed during this period, from heavy and deep to relatively light and shallow.

FAR LEFT, LEFT, AND BELOW LEFT An 18th-century forged-iron door latch; paneled doors hung on hand-forged iron H-hinges; and a pair of plank doors made from wood salvaged from the original structure— all in an 18th-century barn in Harvard, Massachusets, designed and restored by Stephen Mack.

OPPOSITE A pair of fielded-panel doors in an 18th-century Georgian house in Stonington, Connecticut, restored by Stephen Mack. Raised-panel doors became increasingly common from the 1730s onward.

doors ranges from plain deal, pine, and plywood through to teak and mahogany. Plain softwood may be painted or woodgrained, while luxurious hardwoods are more likely to be varnished to show off their natural beauty. As in everything else, styles of door have varied through the centuries, dictated by fashion and

The choice of door finishes and hardware can make an important contribution to the overall decorative scheme of the interior of a room

OPPOSITE AND ABOVE All the doors in the early 19th-century Burr Tavern, in East Meredith, New York, are old and were installed by the present owner. The rustic two-plank cross-battened door (opposite) displays its original buttercup-yellow milk paint, and the more formal four-panel door was recently painted olive green.

ABOVE RIGHT Restored by Stephen Mack, these doors have brass box locks, which were most popular after 1725.

RIGHT A ten-panel arch-top door, flanked by Classical pilasters, in the Federal-style parlor of the Joseph Webb House in Wethersfield, Connecticut.

wealth. Often a period favoring a simple approach is followed by a fashion for more elaborate decoration. In the Victorian period, for example, ready-made pine doors with woodgraining were commonplace, whereas in the later Beaux Arts movement, mahogany became popular, as did French-inspired door panels painted with floral themes, classical trophies, and romantic landscapes. In the early 20th century plywood doors with no paneling or molding were seen as the way forward by Modernists, until architects recognized the role of a door in defining the symmetry of a room. Today, the uniqueness of wood's decorative and design potential is again being exploited to the full.

ABOVE Diamond-pattern cames fixed to iron standards at the Buttolph Williams House, c. 1715, in Wethersfield, Connecticut.

LEFT AND LEFT BELOW The sliding "Indian" shutters in the 18th-century Isaac Stevens House in Wethersfield were designed to block out light and provide privacy and insulation.

FAR LEFT These 12-over-12 sliding sash windows in Chris Ohrstrom's Burr Tavern in East Meredith, New York, have been painted in Spanish brown. As the pigment was locally available, this was an inexpensive color which was traditionally used on woodwork in secondary rooms during the late 18th and early 19th centuries.

RIGHT An upstairs chamber in the 1678 Hempstead House, New London, Connecticut, has original casement leaded windows with diamond-pattern, cames fixed to iron standards (vertical rods).

BELOW RIGHT Two 12-over-12 sash windows allow plenty of light to enter this bedroom at Stephen Mack's 18th-century Chase Hill Farm in Rhode Island.

OPPOSITE, ABOVE LEFT A classic eight-over-eight sash window in The Battery, a late 19th-century wood-framed building in Whitstable, Kent, England, is painted a pastel pink-red to contrast with the pale-blue plank paneling.

A window is much more than a means of letting light into an interior; in most rooms it is a focal point, and the wood chosen for the frame becomes as essential as the view from it.

windows

Early windows were merely unglazed openings in the wall divided by vertical wooden posts (mullions), sometimes with horizontal wooden bars (transoms). The basis for the modern window began in the late 16th century with the availability of glass. The first glass windows were small and fixed in place, but in the 17th century the development of the hinged wooden casement meant they could be opened. Later in the century, vertical-sliding sash windows were invented, allowing larger areas of glass to be opened. In the late 18th century another stylish development in window design was made in the form of French windows, which allowed easy access to outdoors or onto the small balcony of a town apartment. Another important innovation was the bay window, first taking pride of place for front rooms and, later, being used for second-story

windows. Among Modernist architects, vast picture windows were popular. In a secluded rural house a picture window could provide an expansive view of the landscape and greatly enhance the property's value, but in a city it often left the occupants feeling exposed and vulnerable.

Through the centuries, most windows have been framed by wooden surrounds, although with the

RIGHT The bi-fold internal louvered shutters in the Bath House, a modern extension to an early 20th-century wooden house on an island in New Hampshire, were made by the owner.

OPPOSITE Because it has been positioned high up on the Bath House's plank-paneled wall, the louvered trench window admits daylight while providing the privacy for the occupants from the outside.

LEFT Also in the Bath House, the vertical louvers set in this slit-trench window have been designed to swivel open or shut. Sited above showers or baths they have the advantage over stationary louvers of offering additional privacy and enhanced thermal insulation if and when required.

innovative work of Charles Rennie Mackintosh and Frank Lloyd Wright, there was a brief fashion for windows either set flush with the wall surface or recessed without any exterior surround. The Scandinavian influence during the 1930s made wood popular again as a favorite framing material. Traditionally, wooden window frames were protected from the elements with paint or varnish, depending on the wood used. Pine was the obvious choice as it was

cheaper than more desirable hardwoods, but as sealant technology has developed, varnished hardwoods are now used over poorer-quality pine, partly for aesthetic reasons and also because they need less maintenance.

In hot climates, the placement of windows is crucial to create living spaces with enough light, but at the

ABOVE The insertion of a series of large panes of glass in one of the gable ends of this house in Aspen, Colorado, means that plenty of natural light illuminates an upper story open to the Great Hall below.

RIGHT, ABOVE RIGHT, AND OPPOSITE The entrance corridor extends through two storys in a house designed by architect John Mainwaring in Queensland, Australia. Adjustable casement and louvered windows allow the entry of natural light to be controlled and provide good ventilation and an even air-flow so air-conditioning is not needed. At ground level the corridor can be opened to the outside by means of retractable shutters.

Wooden louvered shutters are one way of providing adequate light and ventilation in hot climates, while protecting interior furnishings and providing privacy.

same time to provide much-required protection from the damaging effects of direct sunlight. Wood-framed skylights located in the roof; long, thin windows placed high up in an outside wall; and wooden louvered shutters are just three effective solutions which provide light and ventilation, but protect furniture and upholstery from the sun.

As contemporary architects explore the endless design possibilities that the combination of glass and wood offers, and as ever-improving technology allows thermally efficient glass to cover even greater surface areas, wood-framed windows will continue to be a strong feature of domestic architecture.

built-in furniture

The practicality of built-in shelves and cupboards has guaranteed their continuing popularity.

Built-in furniture was common in early 16th-century Europe and Scandinavia, and the kitchen and dining room were obvious places for storage units. Ventilated food cupboards have always been a natural, practical way of keeping food fresh, and many country properties still incorporate such a unit. Most kitchens had what was known as an aumbry, an enclosed piece of furniture that was created by attaching a frame and doors to a recess in a wall.

Until the end of the 17th century, most Scandinavian interiors featured built-in furniture—walls were honeycombed with beds that were carved and prettily painted. Paneled rooms of the 18th century often had an alcove built into a corner with tiered shelves for displaying china, known as a buffet. Shallow hanging wall cabinets were made during the middle years of the century and corner cupboards had become a familiar fixture. Seats set in window recesses and in areas close to open fireplaces were popular, as were built-in settles with hinged seats to provide storage space. As more books were published, many houses had libraries with built-in shelves. Ranks of drawers and shelves of oak or elm for linen storage were built into the housekeeper's room or in upstairs corridors.

By the early 19th century, high-quality polished hardwoods such as mahogany were popular choices for built-in furniture. Curved corner cupboards were common, and dining rooms often featured a built-in sideboard, cut to fit into a recess in the wall. In libraries, bookshelves were usually sunk within a niche. Relatively little built-in furniture featured during the Regency period through to the 1840s. Kitchens and servants' rooms retained their essential storage spaces, but as carpentry skills improved, furniture was designed as free-standing units. Victorian England saw a burst of growth in built-in

units. Built-in libraries and bedrooms were the height of chic, and a "cozy corner" seating area was often built into a corner or next to a fireplace. A kitchen hutch for storing china was standard. American interiors followed a similar theme.

In the 20th century, the interest in built-in furniture continued to develop, and many architects favored as much furniture as possible being built-in, including cupboards, benches, and beds with shelves or drawers underneath. The practicality of built-in cupboards has ensured their enduring popularity, and built-in kitchens and bathrooms are masterpieces of built-in carpentry, as are bedroom storage units. Yet in a living or dining space, built-ins are out of fashion—we have become a mobile population and like to take our furniture with us when we move on.

ABOVE LEFT The white-painted plank-lined kitchen of Christian Liaigre's house near La Rochelle is furnished simply with bracketed natural-wood open shelving for storage and display, and built-under cupboards with tar-stained pine doors.

TOP RIGHT The bathroom in the late 18th-century Chase Hill Farm contains a free-standing roll-top enameled bathtub, with storage space provided by built-in pine cupboards, pickled and treated with a translucent white stain.

ABOVE The built-in cupboards in the bathroom of the Burr Tavern, East Meredith, New York, were inspired by traditional Shaker designs. The encasement of sanitary fixtures became increasingly fashionable in the 19th century.

furniture

Wooden furniture combining beauty and function has a long tradition, and modern designers still find inspiration in age-old techniques and forms.

The heritage of furniture in a modern country interior can be traced back to the craft traditions of the early carpenters who first took a piece of lumber and transformed it into a chair, a table, or a simple cupboard. Making use of nature's bounty meant taking design cues from natural forms, and early furniture was extremely basic and purely functional. Most furniture designs were evolved by the turner and the joiner, who developed the basic mortise-and-tenon method of joining pieces of wood together. All kinds of wood, but especially oak, elm, and pine were fashioned into practical items, yet each piece yielded its individual beauty to the skill of the craftsman. Although there have been subtle

LEFT AND OPPOSITE On a porch in Aspen, the furniture has been inspired by the rustic furniture of the Adirondacks.

TOP LEFT Rustic forked-branch stools are among the earliest examples of the woodsman's craft, and are common in forested rural areas of Europe, Scandinavia, and the U.S.

TOP RIGHT A pair of "Bruyère" stools in Christian Liaigre's house near La Rochelle, France.

ABOVE Designed by architect Jim Ruscitto, this seat is carved into the top of a large standing-dead pine post that supports the outer edge of an open upstairs gallery in a log house in Aspen, Colorado.

THIS PAGE In this richly colored house in New York state, built c. 1835, a late 18th-century or early 19th-century comb-back rocker from the Boston area retains its original verdigris paint.

changes in construction, modern wooden furniture is derivative of the best design elements of the past and reflects traditions that were perfected over time. Many of the techniques that craftsmen of old persevered to perfect are revered by present-day furniture makers. Contemporary chairs, dining tables, occasional tables, and storage trunks may be made of different types of wood, but the inspiration for their form nearly always comes from the past. The ingenuity of the early colonists has survived technological progress, and much of the modern wooden furniture still produced,

With new, improved tools, skillful carpenters began to design and make more sophisticated, exquisitely crafted free-standing furniture.

either by hand or by small factories around the world, owes its balance and integrity to shapes first seen centuries ago. The fabrics used for upholstery may be more hard wearing, and the wide choice of stain and paint finishes now available are longer lasting, but in the best furniture it is still the shape and grain of the wood that dictate the character of the end piece. Through the centuries a sense of scale has kept designers true to form and use, as they mix old and new designs, combine rough textures with smooth, and incorporate decorations according to fashion.

ABOVE LEFT In the Silas Deane House dining room are chairs from Rhode Island, and a birdcage table from New York, both of mahogany, c. 1760.

ABOVE RIGHT The simple Tibetan-blue painted paneling provides an elegant backdrop for the 19th-century rush-seated country chairs.

RIGHT The furniture in the Washington Bedroom of the Joseph Webb House is typical American Chippendale.

For centuries traditionally crafted wooden objects have been widely appreciated for their natural beauty and sensuality and today, in our age of mass-produced objects, are more highly valued than ever.

OPPOSITE AND BELOW CENTER An Adirondacks-inspired lamp stands on a massive side table hewn from a bark-off tree trunk. The small lamp stand is made from bark-on branches, and the shade is a crudely cut veneer of silver birch bark.

accessories

TOP LEFT A coconut-wood lamp by Donghia Furniture/ Textiles sits on a table in this home on Long Island.

ABOVE The wooden shade for this gas-powered wall lamp was made from cut veneer, steamed and curved into shape.

ABOVE RIGHT A collection of hand-painted Indian treenware sits on a glass-topped cane table in this home on Long Island.

The sensuality of a wooden object is undeniable and its tactile quality compelling: a carved walnut box, polished smooth from years of being handled; simple and functional Shaker boxes for hats, buttons, ribbons, or sewing kit; photograph frames of rough bark; exquisitely carved mirror frames of fragrant wood; painted wooden eggs. It is the texture of the wood as much as the form of the wooden object that is attractive both to look at and to touch. A walking stick of gnarled wood found on a country walk or pieces of driftwood that can be twisted together with twine to make a unique base for a lampshade are perfect accessories for the interior of a wooden house. Nothing is pretentious or out of place, since the craftsman's creation of each item has been inspired by the intrinsic quality of the wood. Since the Industrial Revolution, numerous objects once crafted by hand have been mass-produced by machines, often using synthetic materials. The late 20th century saw a rejection of the bland uniformity of these goods, causing a strong revival of interest in traditionally made wooden objects.

decorating wood

colorwash, paint, and decorative finishes

Over the centuries a variety of washes and paints have been used to color, protect, and decorate the exterior and interior surfaces of timber houses.

Since the early 20th century, pre-mixed oil- and water-based paints, available in an enormous range of colors, have been the favored means of coloring and protecting wooden surfaces. Early painters, however, had to mix their paints and washes on site, making do with locally available ingredients. Limewash is the oldest of the traditional decorative finishes, first used in about 8000 B.C. It is a milklike wash made by slaking lump lime in water to produce lime putty, which is then diluted with water and mixed with a waterproofing agent, such as linseed oil or animal fat. With several coats, it dries to an opaque white color that is

OPPOSITE ABOVE AND BELOW LEFT The Burr Tavern, built in East Meredith, New York, in c. 1835, was originally painted white.

OPPOSITE ABOVE RIGHT To compensate for the power of the sun, Australian architect John Mainwaring employs strong colors on the sub-tropical houses he designs for Queensland's Sunshine Coast.

OPPOSITE BELOW RIGHT The clapboards at the rear of the Bellevue Homestead, Coominya, Australia, are painted a traditional red.

luminous in sunlight, and mat or chalklike when the weather is overcast. Colored limewashes are produced by adding pigments—traditionally earth pigments. Aside from its vibrancy of color, which mellows with age, limewash is semiporous, so any moisture in the surface to which it is applied can evaporate, rather than remain trapped and cause decay. Moreover, the lime works as an antibacterial agent and discourages insect infestation. These aesthetic and physical properties explain its widespread use until the late 19th century. Prior to this time, limewash was also applied to internal walls and woodwork. However, it tended to rub off when brushed against, and so was

ABOVE Prussian blue was a highly fashionable color during the early 19th century. In the Burr Tavern it is used on the stiles of the doors where it contrasts with red oxide molding and yellow ocher panels.

FAR LEFT Along with the rest of the interior, the stairway hall of the late 18th-century Joseph Webb House in Wethersfield, Connecticut, was repainted with oil paints color-matched to the original Georgian green and lilac.

LEFT This hall in the Issac Stevens house, built in 1778–9 in Wethersfield, features fielded paneling and a turned balustrade painted in 18th-century beige drab.

OPPOSITE ABOVE LEFT For the most part, the doors, chimneypiece, ladderback chairs, and "Indian" shutters in the 18th-century Simon Huntington Tavern in Norwich, Connecticut, retain their original milk-paint finishes.

The color of paint chosen for paneling and wood fixtures can dramatically change the atmosphere of a room.

supplanted by whitewash, a simple mixture of whiting (ground, washed chalk) and animal glue, dissolved in water and colored, if desired, with powder pigments. Whitewash dries to give an opaque finish and exhibits a range and an intensity of tones similar to limewash. Yet although it is very effective on plastered walls, it is not especially durable when used on wood, and will soon flake off if the underlying wood has too high a moisture content. Consequently, painters tended to use more resilient media, especially for exposed external wood. These could be oil-based paints, made by grinding earth and mineral pigments into powder and blending them into boiled linseed oil and turpentine, or casein paints, produced by coloring buttermilk or skimmed milk with vegetable or earth pigments usually derived from local plants or clay. Gilding was a popular form of decoration for wooden surfaces, especially paneling and molding. The

ABOVE Here, pale-blue planked walls provide a cool backdrop to a variety of stained and polished woods.

ABOVE FAR LEFT Planked walls in an early 18th-century Norwegian kitchen were repainted in traditional cobalt blue.

ABOVE LEFT The hallway of this house features chamfered-plank walls, and a door and architrave painted in authentic period pink and dark green.

Since the Middle Ages, gilding has been used as a show of opulence.

technique involves sticking thin sheets of gold leaf or gold powder onto wooden or plaster surfaces, and then burnishing them to a shiny, lustrous finish. Since the Middle Ages, gilding has been employed as a show of opulence in many grand houses, applied to the flutes of columns, wooden carvings, wooden and plaster moldings, furniture, mirror frames, and numerous artefacts. In addition to gilding, a variety of specialized techniques have been used to decorate wood. The most popular were stenciling, folk art, woodgraining, and marbling. Stenciling involves transferring patterns and motifs onto a surface by applying paints or dyes through cutouts in a stencil;

ABOVE LEFT This full-height pine chimney wall of raised paneling has been meticulously scraped down to its original blue-green milk paint by restorer Stephen Mack.

RIGHT ABOVE AND BELOW Here, the traditional character of the interior has been retained with flaking white-wash covering the walls, and blue milk paint on the doors.

OPPOSITE The wall paneling and paneled doors in this elegant drawing room in a late 17th-century house in Spitalfields, London, England, are painted dark royal blue and then gilded. The owner has used silver Dutch metal leaf on the large panels, and gold metal leaf on the quadrant moldings.

the patterns used were mainly inspired by rural imagery. Hand-painted folk art allowed unfettered artistic expression and could be decorative or pictorial, drawing on historical, secular, or religious subjects. Developed by the ancient Egyptians, woodgraining is a way of simulating the appearance of wood with paints and glazes on items made of softwood, when hardwood is in short supply. Similarly, marbling, first practiced in Classical times, simulates the appearance of marble and other stones. Like woodgraining, it is still used in areas where the genuine material is

A wide range of natural finishes can be applied to wood to enhance or alter its natural coloring without masking the figuring or grain.

natural finishes

Various stains, varnishes, oils, waxes, and pastes can be applied to wood with the choice depending on the type of wood and the desired effect. For vivid coloring on close-grained softwoods, water-based stains are most suitable, whereas alcohol-based stains result in duller coloring and are most effective on oily hardwoods. Oil-based stains produce the most consistent coloration and are used on fine hardwoods. To protect and enrich stained or unstained wood, modern mat, satin, or gloss polyurethane varnishes are increasingly favored for external and internal woodwork, but traditional alcohol- and oil-based varnishes are still used. On open-grained hardwoods boiled or raw linseed oil is applied instead of varnish, but wax polish is preferred for close-grained hardwoods. To bleach the color of wood, pickling pastes and waxes are used; they also protect the wood. Hardwearing pastes are usually applied to floors and paneling, while less durable waxes are used mainly on furniture.

OPPOSITE The squared-log walls and planked doors in this combined bedroom and bathroom in a restored 18th-century farmhouse in Megève, France, have been pickled and then given additional protection with an application of clear varnish.

ABOVE LEFT AND RIGHT The Hotel Mont-Blanc in Megève was renovated in 1949 by Georges Boisson. The walls of the comfortable bedrooms still retain their original 19th-century pine paneling and pocket doors, which are designed to slide into recesses in the wall. The natural finish of the golden wood creates a feeling of warmth and enhances the attractive markings and grain.

OPPOSITE FAR LEFT AND ABOVE RIGHT The decorative fretwork, in the shape of hearts and flowers, carved scrolls, and ovolo and cyma reversa moldings, displays a fine attention to authentic exterior detail on this "Swiss chalet," built in 1950 in Sun Valley, Idaho.

OPPOSITE BELOW RIGHT Dragon House in Smarden, Kent, England, is a traditional medieval half-timbered house, which had the elaborately decorated dragon frieze added in the 17th century.

RIGHT The Silas Deane House, built in 1766 in Wethersfield, Connecticut, features an open-string staircase with elaborate mahogany balusters.

BELOW RIGHT Tudor-style linenfold paneling on the window shutters of The Green Parlour at Athelhampton House, Dorset, England, a historically important 15th century house.

Decorative carving and turning have featured prominently in wooden houses, their extent and sophistication traditionally an indicator of status.

carving and turning

Hand carving and turning are both highly skilled and time-consuming crafts. Consequently, prior to the advent of mechanised alternatives in the 19th century, the most extensive and intricate examples were largely the preserve of the wealthy. Exteriors and interiors alike have been subject to a vast array of patterns and motifs, ranging from Classical to indigenous Folk Art, from geometric to flora and fauna, from naturalistic to stylized, and all applied to components as diverse as doors, posts, architraves, brackets, beams, panels, and stairs.

index

Note: *italics* refer to captions

A

Abernodwydd Farmhouse, Powys *24–5*

accessories 126, *126–7*

Adirondack Mountains *18, 19–20, 49, 69–70, 122*

aisle framing 23–4

alcohol-based stains 137

alcohol-based varnishes 137

alcoves, built-in furniture 119, *119*

Alps 11, *40*

American Chippendale style *125*

Anguilla *65*

architectural styles 14–35

Art Nouveau 62

Arts and Crafts style 32

furniture 53

lighting *96*

Aspen, Colorado *18, 48–51, 56, 103, 116, 122–3*

Athelhampton House, Dorset *58–9, 61, 62, 106, 137*

attic rooms 94, *118*

Auckland *90–1*

aumbries 119

Australia

decorating wood *130, 131*

floors *98,* 101

weatherboard houses 32–5, *34–5*

windows *116–17*

wood-lined rooms *65, 69, 79, 81, 82, 88–91, 88–9*

Austria 11

B

balconies *40*

balloon framing 12, 31–2, 35

balusters 103, *137*

balustrades 104, *105, 132*

banisters 103

Barfrøstua Farmhouse, Rendalen *66–7*

bark lampshades *127*

barns *94*

Baroque style

paneling 59

staircases 103

basket-framing (balloon framing) 12, 31–2, 35

Bath House, New Hampshire *114–15, 118*

bathrooms, built-in furniture *120*

The Battery, Whitstable Kent *29, 70–1, 112*

bay windows 113

Beaux-Arts style 62, 110

bedrooms, built-in furniture 120

beds, built-in 119

beeswax 68

Bellevue Homestead, Coominya *65, 79, 132*

Bergen, Norway *28, 74–5, 76*

Berriew, Wales *22*

Berrington Manor, Shropshire *24*

bi-fold shutters *115*

Biarritz *102*

birch bark lampshades *127*

birdcage tables *125*

bleaching wood 137

Boisson, Georges *137*

bookshelves *118,* 119

box-framed houses 23, 95

box locks 110

boxes 126

brass locks *110*

brick 29

Brisbane *34, 81, 84–5*

Britain

built-in furniture 119–20

ceilings *95*

decorating wood *135*

doors *106*

half-timbered houses *22–5*

paneling *58–9, 59–61, 62, 63*

weatherboard houses 28, 29, *29*

wood-framed houses *44–5*

wood-lined rooms *69–71*

Brookgate, Shropshire *23, 44–5, 69*

"Bruyère" stools *123*

built-in furniture *118–21, 119–20*

bungalows 35

Burr Tavern, East Meredith, New York *26–7, 104, 110–12, 120, 130, 132*

burrs 54

Buttolph Williams House, Wethersfield, Connecticut *27, 31, 105, 112*

C

cantilevered stairs 103–4, *104*

"Cape Cod" houses *31, 99, 131*

Caribbean *65*

carving *136,* 139

casein (milk) paints 133, *133, 134*

casement windows 113, *133, 116–17*

cedar 82

ceilings 94–7, *95*

paneled *61*

suspended plaster 95

wood-lined rooms 68

chairs 125, *125*

country chairs *125*

ladder-back chairs *133*

rocking chairs *124*

chalets 39

chamfered planks *76–7, 133*

Chase Hill Farm, Rhode Island *31, 99, 104, 107, 108, 113, 120*

Chatel, Megève *17*

china cupboards *118*

chinking *19, 52,* 57

Choseaux, Megève *42*

clapboard see weatherboard houses

Classical style, paneling 59, 62

climate

weatherboard houses 35

and windows 116

closets, built-in *118,* 119–20, *120*

Colonial style

plank cladding 81

stairs *105*

weatherboard houses 29

colors *131*

limewash 131

log-house exteriors 43, 46

log-house interiors 50

paint *132–3*

paneling 62

Shaker style 88

stains 137

wooden floors 98

comb-back rocking chairs *124*

concrete 12

construction methods, wood 11–12

coping method, log houses *52,* 55

corner cupboards 119

country chairs *125*

"country style," wood-lined rooms 69–70

Craftsman style *96*

cross-battened doors 107, *111*

cruck-framed houses 23–4, *44–5,* 95

D

dados 59, 62

Deane (Silas) House, Wethersfield, Connecticut *58–9, 105, 118, 125, 137*

decorating wood

carving and turning *138–9,* 139

log houses 43–6

natural finishes *136–7,* 137

paint 130–5, *131–4*

Delft, Ischa van *78,* 119

dining rooms, built-in furniture 119

dining tables 125

dog-leg staircases 103, *104, 105*

Donghia Furniture/Textiles *126*

door furniture *108*

doors 106–11, *107–10*

cross-battened 107, *111*

"double-boarded" 68, 107, *107*

acknowledgments

The author and
publisher would
like to thank the
following people for
their invaluable help
in the preparation
of this book:

Rodney Archer
Donna Baron
Jonathan and
  Pauline Barres
Marina and Bill
  Beadleston

Peter Beale
Dr Tom and
  Mrs Pat Bell
Don and Anne
  Cameron
Frank and Suz
  Cameron
Cathy Capri
Simon and Robyn
  Carnachan
Jim and Hilda
  Chapman
Patrick Cooke
Carolyn Davies

Ischa van Delft
Sherri Donghia and
  Robert Eulau
Priscilla Endicott
Dave Fritchley
Kevin and Sue
  Godley
Olav Golid
Jolie and Petrea
  Grant
Isak I Grave
Annie Har and
  William Hayes
Sue and Dick Hare

Happy Hawn
Astrid Poulsson
  Hesledalen
Hallgrim Høydal
Jon Geir and Inger
  Høyersten
Angela Kent
Richard Lewis and
  Donna Allen
Christian Liaigre
Holly Lueders and
  Richard Spizzirri
Rob and Sarah
  McConnell

Stephen P Mack
John Mainwaring
Alf and Wendy
  Martensson
Graham Moss
Bergit Myrjord
Gerallt D Nash
Chris Ohrstrom
Marilyn Phipps
Alan and Marion
  Powell
Mark Pynn
Michèle Rédélé

Anna and Halvor
  Rekaa
Margaret Rogers
Jim Ruscitto
Allan Shope
Jocelyne and Jean
  Louis Sibuet
Philip and Barbara
  Silver
Jørgen H Sønstebø
Tone Stivi
Kare Sveen
Tony Suttle
Olivier Vidal

credits

Grateful thanks to the following architectural, building and interior design companies whose houses and work is featured in this book:

Allan Shope (Architect)

Shope Reno Wharton Associates
18 West Putnam Avenue
Greenwich
CT 06830
+1 203 869 7250
Fax: +1 203 869 2804
www.shoperenowharton.com
Pages 72, 73, 103l

Angela Kent (Architect)

Kenström Design Pty Ltd
92 Cathedral Street
Woolloomooloo
NSW 2011
Australia
Pages 14–15, 88–89, 98r

Annie Har

Sunnit Architects
10 Attunga Lane
Mount Glorious
Queensland 4520
Australia
Page 69bl

Athelhampton House

Athelhampton
Dorchester
Dorset DT2 7LG
UK
www.athelhampton.co.uk
Pages 10ar, 58al, 58br, 59a, 61al, 61ar, 61b, 62ar, 106, 139b

Chris Ohrstrom

Historic Paints Ltd
Burr Tavern
Route 1, PO Box 474
East Meredith
New York NY 13757
www.adelphipaperhangings.com
Pages 26, 27a, 101br, 104al, 110al, 111, 112bl, 120br, 124, 130al, 130bl, 132a

Christian Liaigre (Furniture and interior designer)

www.christian-liaigre.fr
Pages 12a, 80, 82, 96a, 105bl, 107bl, 120l, 121, 123ar

Glomdalsmuseet

Museum for Østerdalen and Solor
Glomdalsmuseet
Postboks 1270
N-2405 Elverum
Norway
www.glomdal.museum.no
Pages 20–21, 66–67, 123ac

Graham Moss (Specialist conservator of early buildings, architectural, constructional and decorative finishes.)

Moss Co Architects
Brookgate
Plealey
Shrewsbury SY5 0UY
UK
Pages 23al, 23ac, 23bl, 24l, 44, 45, 69r, 107al, 107r

Holly Lueders Design (Building, interior and furniture design)

450 West 31st Street
New York NY
Pages 6, 10al, 18al, 18bl, 48, 49, 50, 51, 122l, 122–123 main

Hotel Mont-Blanc
Place de l'Église;
Les Fermes de Marie
Chemin de Riante Colline;
Les Fermes des Grand Champ
Choseaux
74120 Megève
France
Pages 1, 13a, 17a, 18–19, 42, 43, 68, 69al, 137 both

Ischa van Delft (Interior decorator)

September
Vughterstraat 72
5211 GK's-Hertogenbosch
Holland
Pages 78, 98l, 119l, 125ar

Jim Ruscitto (Architect)

Ruscitto, Latham, Blanton
PO Box 419
Sun Valley
Idaho ID 83353
Pages 52–55, 56–57 main, 57a, 57b, 92–93, 123b, 126ac, 127

John Mainwaring & Associates

JMA Architects qld
Level 1, 36 Wyandra St
Newstead
Brisbane
Queensland 4006
Australia
+61 7 3252 4400
fax +61 7 3252 2911
www.jma-arch.com
Pages 35, 116ar, 116b, 117, 130ar

Mark Pynn (Architect)

www.sunvalleyarchitect.com
Sun Valley
Idaho ID 83353
Pages 4–5, 32–33, 96b both, 97, 105br

Michael Fuller Architects

Colorado
(formerly Conger Fuller Architects)
www.mfullerarchitects.com
Pages 8–9, 10b, 56l, 103ar, 103br, 116al

Michèle Rédélé (Interior designer)

90 Boulevard Malegerbes
Paris 75008
France
Pages 17b, 38–39, 39, 40, 41, 94al, 136

Museum of Welsh Life

St Fagan's
Cardiff CF5 6XB
Wales
Pages 24–25, 95 both

Olivier Vidal and Associates (Architects)

14 rue Moncey
75009 Paris
France
Pages 11b, 86–87, 104b

Rob and Sarah McConnell (Builder and paint specialist)

8 Coastguard Cottages
Coastguard Square
Rye Harbour
East Sussex TN31 7TS
UK
in conjunction with
Dave Fritchley
(Log detailing/twig work and rustic furniture specialist)
Eggshole Cottage
Starvecrow Lane
Peasmarsh
East Sussex TN3 16XN
UK
Page 11a

Simon Carnachan
Carnachan Architects Ltd.
(Architects, interior designers and landscape architects)

Level 1
15 Bath Steet
Parnell
Auckland
New Zealand
09 302 0222
Fax 09 302 0234
www.carnachan-architects.co.nz
Pages 2, 90–91

Steven Conger Architects

Colorado
(formerly Conger Fuller Architects)
www.congerarchitects.com
Pages 8–9, 10b, 56l, 103ar, 103br, 116al

Stephen P Mack

A nationally renowned designer and expert in the restoration and reconstruction of 17th- and 18th-century structures and their environs.
Stephen P Mack Associates
Chase Hill Farm
Ashaway
Rhode Island RI 02804
www.stephenpmack.com
Home of Stephen P Mack: 31a, 99, 104ar, 107ac, 108al, 108ar, 113b, 120ar, 131ar, 133al, 134ar, 134br
Work of Stephen P Mack: 29al, 29bc, 58ar, 60–61, 94ar, 108bl, 108cr, 108br 109, 110ar, 134l

The Buttolph Williams House

249 Broad Street
Wethersfield
Connecticut CT 06109
www.hartnet.org/ALS
Pages 27b, 31b, 105cr, 112ar

The Hempstead House

11 Hempstead Street
New London
Connecticut CT 06320
www.hartnet.org/ALS
Page 113a

The National Trust Queensland

National Trust House
95 William Street, Brisbane
Queensland
Australia
www.nationaltrustqld.org
Bellevue Homestead, Coominya:
Pages 7, 65a, 65b, 78, 131bl,
Mayes Cottage, Logan (managed by Logan City Council): 130br

The Webb-Deane-Stevens Museum

211 Main Street
Wethersfield
Connecticut CT 06109
www.webb-deane-stevens.org
Pages 3, 30, 58bl, 59b, 62br, 94b, 105al, 105ar, 110b, 112cr, 112br, 118bl, 118br, 125al, 125b, 132bl, 132br, 139a

Tony Suttle

Woods Bagot Pty Ltd
Architects
64 Marine Parade
Southport
Queensland 4215
Australia
Pages 34, 84–85